DAWDLING THROUGH THE

DALES

John Morrison

Halsgrove

First published by Halsgrove in 2003

British Library Cataloguing-in-Publication Data
A CIP record for this title is available from the British Library

ISBN 1 84114 278 6

HALSGROVE
Halsgrove House
Lower Moor Way
Tiverton EX16 6SS
T: 01884 243242
F: 01884 243325
www.halsgrove.com

Printed in Great Britain by
The Cromwell Press, Trowbridge

*Author's note to readers who might easily be
offended…This book contains a good deal of 'robust'
humour. Don't blame the publishers, the fault is mine
alone. Let's put it down to hormonal imbalance; the male
menopause can be a difficult time.*

INTRODUCTION

By John Morrison

B efore I walked the Dales Way I was working on another book, *Fifty Walks in Yorkshire*. A pleasant enough activity, except that walking in fifty small circles seemed rather too accurate a metaphor for my life in general. I've written quite a few other walking books, but the publishers of this one had very strict ideas about what they wanted. Every walk in the book – fifty, count 'em, fifty – were to have detailed route descriptions, and be graded in all sorts of pointless ways. Gradient, ease of walking, 'dog friendliness', number of stiles encountered on the way, places to eat and drink, where to put your feet to avoid piles of dog shit: that sort of guff and a great deal more.

The book had to be filled with fatuously obvious information, such as: don't walk without proper clothing. Wear boots, not carpet slippers. Take a map. Pack some sandwiches. Stay upright; don't fall over. If you do fall over, get up again. Put one foot in front of the other until you get to point A. Slip tab B into slot C and… well, you get the picture. The target readership for this book? It was for people whose idea of a stiff walk seemed to be a lateral traverse of Tesco's car park.

This is what most walking books are like these days: dreary and utilitarian. My author's notes – page after page of them – precluded any passages of description. Adjectives were forbidden; enthusiasm too. A to B and back again: that was the be-all and end-all. But for all their nannying and hand-holding, most walking books have one major drawback. If, despite all the instructions, a reader *does* happen to get lost, these books offer no guidance for rejoining the path. The sketch-maps are just that… sketches. And the writers of walking guides are notoriously unreliable (if you see a guy with the words 'left' and 'right' painted on the toecaps of his boots, you can guess what he does for a living). Yes, if the reader makes one wrong turn –

whether through his own fault, or the writer's poor route descriptions – he is not merely lost, but hopelessly and irredeemably lost.

What every walker needs, whether he carries a walking book or not, is the appropriate set of Ordnance Survey maps. Let's get it straight: every walk in every walking book is already featured on one Ordnance Survey map or another. You know it. I know it. Most of the people who fork out folding money for walking books must know it too. All the writer has done is trace it out, walk the route (if he's had the time and inclination) and given it some fatuous name. In the Footsteps of the Brontës, or something similar. But still the books sell, albeit with diminishing returns.

While I'm no great fan of walking books, I would like to raise my glass to the Ordnance Survey map: an invaluable resource that we walkers tend to take for granted. If I don't have the appropriate OS map in my rucksack, I don't feel quite dressed for a walk. It's always the first item in my rucksack. I know it's a bugger to fold. I know it turns to unreadable mush in the rain. I know that the place you want to find is invariably on the wrong side of a double-sided map. But in a world of mediocrity (yes, most of those walking books again, I'm afraid), the OS map shines as a beacon of excellence.

I'm lucky. Even on the rainiest of days I have a way of 'escaping' to the great outdoors. While some folk curl up with a big, fat winter book (one of those family sagas, perhaps, as big as a house brick), I read maps. Yes, whenever I hear the clarion call of the countryside – but can't resist the soft siren voice of the sofa – I spread out an OS map on the living room carpet. Then, as the *Yellow Pages* adverts used to suggest, I let my fingers do the walking.

I enjoy getting lost – not in the twists and turns of some Byzantine plot, but in the swirling patterns of contour lines that typify the northern uplands. I don't need to switch on the computer to experience 'virtual reality'. A map does the job every bit as well.

I plan new routes, and revisit walks I've done before. Tracing a stubby finger along those hatched green lines, I relive every foot-slogging mile, every lung-bursting climb, every stale cheese and pickle sandwich. As I sprawl over a 1:25,000 version of my favourite landscapes, I experience once again the sights, sounds, smells and tastes of the countryside. The flash of blue as a kingfisher takes wing. The song of the skylark. The smell of wild garlic in the woods. A jumbo sausage, chips and peas in one of the few pubs where I can still find a welcome.

Anyway, as a reward for finishing those fifty circular walks, I promised myself a longer walk in a straight line. The Dales Way, beginning at Ilkley and ending at the shores of Lake Windermere, looked like the ideal choice for a free week in October. It seemed an auspicious time: a week wedged between blackberry-picking and Bonfire Night, just before the clocks went back.

The route passes through some of the most beautiful countryside in England, but, unlike the Pennine Way (the grandaddy of long-distance walks), it doesn't require too much hard work, slogging pointlessly through peat bogs. And the Dales Way has a defined finishing point. When you're up to your boot-tops in the waters of Windermere, you know you can stop walking.

The boots were well worn in, thank goodness, but I had bought a smart new backpack for the trip. Oh, and a mobile phone. I'd held off buying a mobile for a long time, so I wouldn't ever be tempted to phone someone merely to tell them I was on a train. But the walk provided me with the excuse I needed to join the happy band of phone users. If I were to break a leg half way up a mountain, think how useful it would be to call the rescue service. Without a mobile, who – apart from grouse and curlew – would hear my piteous cries?

I had a comprehensive list of places to stay, from primitive bunk-barns to smart hotels (*The Dales Way Handbook*: full of useful information, updated every year, and a snip at £1.50). I thought how convenient it would be, each day, to phone ahead and arrange a bed for the night, thus ensuring that I had a place to lay my weary head. Anyway, I got a special deal from Virgin for being the last person in the universe to own a mobile phone. When, in an attempt to keep the weight of my rucksack down, I had to choose between the phone and a torch, I plumped for the phone. It seemed like the right thing to do.

If you plan to walk the Dales Way, be assured that the book you are holding will not help you follow the route. There are a number of slim, pocketable books that *will*, some of them written by Colin Speakman, whose brainchild the Dales Way largely was. My book may whet your appetite for the walk, or bring back a few memories once you have completed it. Better yet, put your feet up, plump up those sofa cushions, make yourself comfortable and consider the book as a substitute for doing the walk at all.

LEEDS TO ILKLEY

The Cow and Calf Rocks   Jim Watson

It was a Friday morning in late October when I laced up my walking boots and caught the train to Leeds. Leeds used to promote itself – with perverse pride – as 'The Motorway City of the Seventies', even though it made no more sense than branding it 'The Anthrax City of the Eighties', or 'The Nuclear City of the Nineties'. The country's first motorway, the M1, was driven in a ruler-straight line (the Romans would have been proud) from the outskirts of London to Yorkshire, and right into the heart of Leeds. Back then motorways were seen as the solution to our traffic ills, not part of the problem. The more motorways we had the better, with the result that South Leeds is now a bewildering maze of motorway spurs and flyovers that baffle all but the savviest motorists.

Having defined itself by this labyrinthine road system, Leeds now tries to sell itself on sophistication. The city's new status, as a smart, 'happening' kind of place, has been rubber-stamped, apparently, by the opening of a branch of Harvey Nichols. This may mean something to you, dear reader, but I'm a man who buys his clothes from charity shops (you would know that if you met me) so it means bugger-all to me.

The original vision for the Dales Way was as a footpath from Woodhouse Moor to Lake Windermere, a distance of nearly 100 miles. Though Ilkley became the 'official' starting point, the 'Woodhouse Moor to Windermere' idea lives on in the form of a link path. There are three link paths – giving walkers the choice to start from Leeds, Bradford or Harrogate. My choice was Leeds, because it gave me a chance to wander down Memory Lane and bemoan the fact that 'Everything's changed since I were a lad. I can remember when all this was fields.' And who wants to pass up an opportunity like that?

So I took a bus to Woodhouse Moor: about a mile from the centre of Leeds and an old haunt of mine. When the fair came to town, it came to Woodhouse Moor. It was here, as a boy, that I saw one of the last freak shows to tour the country. Well, I *hope* it was one of the last. There were two-headed calves, six-legged sheep, honest politicians and other mythical beasts, all pickled in formaldehyde.

The fair was seedy, grubby and seductively disreputable, drawing me towards the flashing lights and discordant music, like a moth to a flame. For a young lad from the suburbs, it was like a day-trip to Sodom and Gomorrah. I can remember the studied indifference of the guys with the Elvis quiffs who worked the waltzers; the girls spinning around, so dizzy they didn't know whether to scream or to laugh. Guys hopped nonchalantly from one car to another, in the middle of dodgem carnage, to collect the money. Music blasted out, at migraine-inducing volume, from tinny speakers on every ride and stall: an exhilarating cacophony designed to shake the punters' fillings out of their teeth, and the pennies from their pockets.

Stalls were piled high with sugary confections: popcorn, peanut brittle, ginger snaps and toffee apples. They proved to be an equally effective (though longer-term) strategy for rotting kids' teeth into blackened stumps. Pink candyfloss was spun onto sticks in a bouffant shape that became the inspiration for Dusty Springfield's elaborate coiffure. I recall the smell of Westler's hamburgers (they came in tins and were boiled, not fried) which my libel lawyers insist are made of prime beef and nothing but prime beef... plus maybe a pinch of seasoning. Mmmm, I can almost smell them now. Unless it's the drains.

Kids tried to toss ping-pong balls into goldfish bowls, hoping to win a goldfish in a little plastic bag: a convenient way to teach children about pet-care and mortality, often on the same day. And the shooting range: so mindlessly simple that no one sober enough to stand upright could fail to claim a prize. After half a dozen wins, the stallholder would direct your gaze – with an airy wave of the hand – towards 'anything on the bottom shelf'. That would be a whistle, or a novelty key-ring, or a plastic 'glow-in-the-dark' skeleton.

The fair still comes to Woodhouse Moor. Amazingly, in a world where the only constant seems to be change, the fair looks, sounds and smells much the same as it did when I was a kid. The music may be different but, since it's played through those same tinny speakers, who can be sure?

I was enjoying my little stroll down Memory Lane, on a sunny autumn day. When I used to live here – in bedsit land – I was young, hopelessly naive and with no more sense than God gave geese. After a childhood in the leafy suburbs, the terrraced streets of Leeds seemed almost unbearably exotic. Indian women sat on doorsteps, shading their eyes – purely out of habit – against cloud-filled English skies. I frequented pubs where men with broken noses stood at the bar and supped pints of Tetley's Bitter.

It was here, just a short walk from the university, that I first sampled academia and Bohemia (that's a land that shares a common border with academia) and the arcane delights of sharing a semi-derelict house with loose women and drug-addled strangers. Of course, dealing cannabis was a rather more gentlemanly pursuit than it is today. And a 'quid deal' of Lebanese Red was so big that you could barely squeeze it into a shoebox.

I lived in squalor (it's twinned with Bohemia): a cramped bedsit on the ground floor. Mad Jack lived in the next room which – from a blessedly brief inspection – seemed to be full of unwashed pots and semen-spattered underpants. Jack worked at the local swimming baths; in what capacity I shudder to imagine. Whenever I got a female visitor, a hairy arm would reach out and drag the unsuspecting lass into his lair. Alerted by the screams, I'd knock on Jack's door and ask for my visitor back, before he had a chance to find his chloroform-soaked handkerchief.

On this October morning, I stood for a few respectful seconds outside another modest terraced house nearby. It was here that I lost my virginity. There is nothing – to the untrained eye, at least – that distinguishes the house from its neighbours, or acknowledges those momentous events from so long ago. There is no blue plaque, no inscription. What was it like? It was splendid, and thank you for asking.

Nowadays, this area of Leeds is full of wacky little shops selling second-hand tapes and CDs. I was about to walk into one when I was stopped by a guy coming out. 'You don't want to go in there,' he smirked, 'It's all dance music. You know: jungle, techno, garage.' '*I* dance,' I lied, a bit sniffy about being pigeonholed so easily (and so very accurately).

Yes, no matter where you go, Memory Lane is a cul-de-sac. It was time to start my walk. Pulling my fleecy hat down over my ears, I walked down Raglan Road, on an autumn day, through streets of red-brick terraced houses, and up to Woodhouse Ridge.

The fun of starting a walk from here is that a narrow corridor of wooded greenery – now being promoted as the Meanwood Valley Trail – extends almost into the heart of Leeds. OK, it's no Serengeti, but it's still a pleasant surprise to find such rural surroundings wedged between the terraces, the old mills, the industrial units, the allotments and the unplanned clutter of city life. In a far-sighted

10

move, Leeds Corporation bought Woodhouse Moor in 1855, and Woodhouse Ridge a few years later. Mainly open pasture at that time, with a network of footpaths, the ridge was subsequently laid out as a public park. The legacy of these purchases – and many others – is that Leeds now has more public open space per head of population than any other city in Europe. And that, Mr Harvey Bleeding Nichols, is something worth celebrating.

I passed the backs of substantial stone houses in Headingley. This was one of the city's first suburbs: a haven for those who'd made their brass in less salubrious parts of Leeds. And just because they'd made their brass from the proverbial muck, that didn't mean they had to live right on top of it. When Charles Dickens condemned Leeds as 'One of the nastiest places I know,' I don't think he had Headingley in mind.

Headingley is, of course, the home of Yorkshire County Cricket Club. The ground has witnessed some titanic battles – mostly, it must be said, between the committee members. The 'Blazerati' – intractable Yorkshiremen of impeccable character – have provided the rest of the country with a good deal of harmless (though unintentional) amusement over the years. There was a vicarious thrill in watching a cricket club implode into rancorous factions, not least because it was all done so very publicly. It was, at any rate, more fun than watching Yorkshire CCC lose to all-comers at every time of asking.

It wasn't always like this. Under the autocratic leadership of Lord Hawke – captain from 1883 to 1910 – Yorkshire began a domination of the County Championship that arguably lasted until the 1970s. (The championship Yorkshire won as recently as 2001 is already looking like a bizarre aberration – due, perhaps, to a fortuitous rupture in the space/time continuum, or was it all just a dream? – since it was immediately followed by relegation.)

Even though he himself was born in Lincolnshire, Lord Hawke insisted that only Yorkshire-born cricketers could play for the county. Then, as now, there was one rule for the nobs and another for everybody else. His teams were made up of amateur 'gentlemen' and professional 'players'. And, just in case the social divide was not sufficiently obvious, the gentlemen had one changing room and the players had another. At a club dinner in 1925, Lord Hawke secured his place in the book of sporting quotations with this heartfelt cry: 'Pray God that no professional may ever captain England!' The amateur distinction was formally abandoned as recently as 1962; after this date all first-class players were known simply as cricketers.

For players who did not share Lord Hawke's social standing, the Yorkshire-only rule lasted a hundred years. If the stories are to be believed, pregnant women were driven at speed, back over the county line, so that a boy child might one day be eligible to play for the county. I myself had all the requisite qualifications, except the one that really mattered: cricketing talent.

It's all changed now, and Yorkshire have dispensed with the one and only rule that made them stand out from the crowd. Anyone can play for Yorkshire now.

It's wonderful to spend a sunny day watching test cricket at Headingley. For a generation raised on MTV and the three-minute culture, it may seem a rather anachronistic pastime. But you can have a few beers and doze for an hour; then you wake up, blinking myopically into the sunshine, your shirt-front covered in snail-trails of dribble, secure in the knowledge that you've missed nothing of importance.

I remember when Geoffrey Boycott was approaching the milestone of his hundredth first-class hundred. An unmitigated bore he may be these days, but back then, in 1977, he couldn't half bat. With characteristic timing he decided that this landmark feat should be performed in the Queen's jubilee year, against the Australians, in front of a partisan Yorkshire crowd at Headingley. It's strange to recall a time when an England batsman could orchestrate the highpoints of his career in such a way, but then Geoffrey Boycott always did march to a different drum. In the previous game, at Trent Bridge, he'd created test match history in a typical Boycott way: by being at the crease at some point during all five days of a test match.

A mate of mine, who lived next to the ground, invited me to witness the great event. At the bottom of his garden was a flat-roofed shed, just big enough to support a couple of deckchairs. It was as good a vantage point as you'd get from inside the ground; better yet, it was free. In gratitude, but forgetting he was teetotal, I brought two six-packs of beer to share. That meant I had a dozen cans of industrial-strength lager all to myself.

Well, sunshine, beer and test cricket are a potent combination, and the excitement mounted as Geoffrey accumulated his runs. By the time he had reached the 'nervous nineties,' I was in expansive mood. As he stroked the ball to the boundary for his century, and waved his bat in the air, I felt the need to share in the celebrations. I clambered over the barbed wire – with no thought for my personal safety – and into the cricket ground. As John Arlott was delivering a well-rehearsed paean to Cooff's cricketing achievements, he broke off just long enough to lambast some drunken young fools for running out into the middle and shaking the centurion by the hand. Well, I'm immensely proud to say that one of those drunken young fools was me.

Geoffrey went on to make 191 out of a first innings total of 436. England won the match by an innings and 85 runs, and the series 3-0, thus retaining the Ashes. Hooray!

I walked on good paths, through ginnels and snickets, following Meanwood Beck, until I came to another of my old stamping grounds. It is a tiny cricket ground – quite a contrast to Headingley – shoehorned between two streams, an old mill and Meanwood Park. The water was so close on both sides that a lofted pull or cover drive required the ball to be retrieved with the child's fishing net that was always to hand.

I went misty-eyed to see where I first played school cricket. Yes, there was a time when cricket was a healthy interest for me, rather than the all-consuming obsession it is today. However, the one image that's ingrained in my memory isn't of me performing heroically with ball or bat. On one particular summer afternoon the kids who weren't playing were forced to watch the game. This merely reinforced what they already believed: that cricket was boring, and that being made to watch a game was some kind of punishment. So, naturally enough, their attention was apt to wander away from the less-than-riveting contest taking place on the pitch. And, as if on cue, a horse in an adjoining paddock was starting to feel frisky. So frisky, in fact, that its tumescent todger was dragging along the ground. We'd never seen anything like it: dark brown, almost black, it looked as though it had been sculpted from teak.

The teachers tried their best to bring everyone's attention back to the game. But let's face facts. What would you rather watch: twenty-two flannelled fools playing an inter-school cup match, or a horse with a monumental hard-on? I thought so. It was an apt metaphor for one of cricket's biggest problems: how to make the sport more popular in the face of so many competing distractions.

From Meanwood Park and a row of cottages called, intriguingly, Hustlers Row, the path entered The Hollies – still part of the wooded Meanwood Valley – before ducking beneath the tarmacadam tourniquet that is the Leeds Ring Road. Adel Woods provided something that looked less like an urban park, and more like a bit of proper countryside. It was here, eons ago, that I used to play with a gang of lads. A girl called Melanie used to hang around too; one day we pushed her into Meanwood Beck. She went home in tears, soaked to the skin; then she came straight back, in clean clothes. So we pushed her in the beck again. Ah, yes, happy days.

When I say 'gang,' I don't want to give the impression that we were tough, street-hardened kids. We took our inspiration from Enid Blyton's Famous Five, rather than the vicious street gangs of the Lower East Side of Los Angeles. That made us a particularly unfearsome bunch of desperados. But what we lacked in weaponry, we made up for in resourcefulness.

We built dens in these woods: artless clumps of brushwood to the casual observer, but impregnable fortresses to us. We were prepared, at any moment, to be attacked by wholly imaginary foes: difficult adversaries to defend against. We rooted out crime, even where there was none, and investigated all kinds of suspicious happenings.

One day we found a car parked up on a woodland track, with its windows steamed up. We heard screams, but that was only *after* we'd peered in. We saw a man digging in the woods. Assuming, naturally enough, that he was burying one of his murder victims in a shallow grave, we shadowed his every move. The alternative scenario – that he was just bagging up leaf-mould for his garden – seemed too far-fetched.

Our gang became quorate, in a strict Enid Blyton sense, by the addition of Kim, a playful labrador. Though enthusiastic, she didn't fully understand the role we had earmarked for her, which was to initiate all kinds of new adventures. Being loyal fans of Lassie and Rin Tin Tin on TV, we knew how much fun a dog could be. So whenever Kim wagged her tail we were ready to say those immortal words: 'Look, I think Kim's trying to tell us something. She wants us to follow her down to the old barn.'

Ignoring what she really wanted – a tummy-rub, perhaps, or a tin of butcher's tripe – we would all troop after her. Not to buried treasure, alas. Nor to the scene of some unspeakable crime which we – and not some bungling oaf of a policemen – would manage to solve. No, Kim would generally lead us to a dead sheep, quietly putrefying in the corner of a field. 'Good dog,' we'd say – not wanting to hurt her feelings, but not thinking too clearly either. It taught Kim one thing only: that we wanted her to find more dead sheep.

I made the first of many deviations from the 'official' Dales Way, to pass the accurately named Five Lane Ends and enter Golden Acre Park, near Bramhope. The park – actually 137 acres in total, and in no sense golden – was created, back in 1930, as an amusement park. It wasn't just a few swings either, but a veritable Yorkshire Disneyland. Visitors could ride the miniature railway for almost 2 miles; there was even a dining car. They could test their nerves on the 'Mountain Glide' or take a motor boat trip around the lake. They could watch races by the Yorkshire Hydroplane Racing Squadron. And the Winter Gardens Dance Hall boasted 'the largest dance floor in Yorkshire'.

But despite all these many attractions, the people of Leeds did not flock to the park in sufficient numbers. By 1938 it had closed. Leeds City Council made another prescient purchase, in 1945, and gradually transformed Golden Acre Park from an amusement park into formal gardens and a wildlife sanctuary. The only remnants of the park's previous incarnation was the lake and an open-air lido known, rather imaginitively, as The Blue Lagoon, which offered unheated swimming and the prospect of goose-pimples. I only got the chance to swim on a few occasions in those less-than-limpid waters before the pool was drained for the last time. Bathers who wanted to catch crabs or impetigo were forced to make alternative arrangements.

A short walk around the park offers a variety of habitats for attracting birds: woods, heathland and quarry. The lake is the most obvious focus, with a resident flock of waterfowl. An identification board helps to put names to the ducks, geese, gulls and swans that come to gorge themselves on visitors' bread. Great crested grebes perform elaborate mating rituals during the breeding season. Whooper swans fly down from Scandinavia to winter here. There is probably nowhere else in West Yorkshire where you could spot so many species of birds in so small an area. It is quite a surprise to find this oasis within the Leeds city boundary.

I left Golden Acre Park by a short tunnel beneath the busy A660 road, and entered Breary Marsh: one of West Yorkshire's few remaining wetlands. Access through the alder woods is on raised wooden duckboards; more information panels help to identify the flora and fauna. At the far end of Breary Marsh is the tranquil little mere known as Paul's Pond. I spotted a heron, moving slowly, stealthily, deliberately, in a way that any martial arts enthusiast would immediately recognise as t'ai chi. I made a circuit of the pond, before following field-paths into Bramhope.

This is where I was born and brought up. It used to be a proper village and, if you stand at the memorial cross at the top of the hill, by the Fox and Hounds, the chippy and a little cluster of shops, and half close your eyes, you can vaguely imagine how it might have looked a hundred years ago. But Bramhope has proved to be such an agreeable place to live – within easy commuter range of the city, yet backing onto open fields – that it has spread over the landscape to the north of Leeds like an itchy rash.

Town planners would probably call it a dormitory suburb. It's always been rather posh – saying 'I'm from Bramhope' is an effective conversation killer round these parts. It's hard to believe you're in West Yorkshire. Bramhope is a quiet place, for people who've either made it in business or who want to spend their declining years in comfortable surroundings.

Life in Bramhope was unexciting; it was meant to be. No doubt there were displays of passion played out behind those velvet curtains, but they never spilled out onto the streets. People laughed and cried behind locked doors. It wouldn't occur to anyone to nip next door to borrow a cupful of sugar. No one played their music loud. No one staggered drunkenly home from the pub and then beat his wife. If there was any wife-beating going on, it would have been conducted with discretion and decorum. There would have been no need to disturb the neighbours. That's the kind of place Bramhope is: a convincing dress-rehearsal for being dead.

I set my pack down in the Fox and Hounds, for old times' sake, and had a quick pint and a sandwich. I was glad to be leaving Bramhope. There are good reasons why we avoid the place where we grew up, and mine were starting to come back to me.

Having crossed the A658 Leeds-Harrogate road, I strolled through conifer woodland – the firebreaks between the rows of trees providing tantalising glimpses of the valley beyond. The walking terrain had been pretty flat so far, but the contour lines were squeezed more closely together as I approached the Chevin: an exposed gritstone escarpment that offers panoramic views over Lower Wharfedale and the little town of Otley. It's here that Dales Wayfarers have their first view of the Wharfe – a river they will get to know rather better over the next few days.

Otley Chevin (or, more grandly, the Chevin Forest Park) has long been a popular spot. In 1944 a Major Fawkes of nearby Farnley Hall gave a piece of land on the Chevin to the people of Otley. By 1989, when it was designated a local nature reserve, the Chevin Forest Park had grown to 700 acres of woodland, heath and gritstone crags. Local people come here to walk their dogs, and the broad forest tracks are ideal for mountain bikers and horse riders.

On this particular afternoon, all the horse riders seemed to be young and female. I moved aside, with a cheery wave, to let them trot by. The attraction of horses is something I don't really understand. But there are so many other, more important things I don't understand that it's not a problem. I've always assumed that girls must get a degree of sensual gratification from horses – in a steamy, leathery, muscular, DH Lawrence kind of way. If you mention this, in passing, to most horsewomen, they get rather sniffy. There's nothing sexual, they insist, about their passion for horses. But another woman, breaking ranks, has told me, in lascivious confidence, that, by jingo, there *is*. So I'm still none the wiser.

People flock to the Chevin, and particularly the car park at Surprise View. There's a pub nearby, The Royalty: one of those solitary pubs, in the middle of nowhere, that you find all over West Yorkshire. This gives punters everything they require of a day out, which, according to one of my more cynical chums in the tourism business, is 'a view, a brew and a loo'. The view, at least, is splendid. Almscliffe Crag is a prominent landmark in the valley: a pimple on an almost ruler-straight horizon. On a clear day you may be able to see Simon's Seat, and even the famous White Horse carved into the hillside at Kilburn. With a view like this, it's easy to forget that you are little more than a mile away – as the crow flies – from the bustle of the Leeds-Bradford Airport.

The view on this bright October day was no big surprise for me. The Chevin is another familiar haunt. I used to come here with a chum who designed, built and flew his own radio-controlled gliders. The slope of the Chevin descends in a smooth curve into the valley, and, on days when the wind blew from the north, model planes would get plenty of lift. It was wonderful to launch them from the top of the ridge, and see them soar out over Wharfedale until they were little more than specks in the sky, before bringing them back over our heads with a twiddle of the controls. The gliders would lose height as they quartered the heath and heather behind us, then Howard would fly them back over the ridge again; straight out into the teeth of the wind with a force that should have torn his planes to pieces… and sometimes did.

Best of all was interacting with the birds. It was magical when the plane attracted the aerobatic attentions of a kestrel – or maybe that same proverbial crow – when bird and plane would glide and swoop as one. It was almost like we were talking to the birds. And it stayed that way until I got my medication changed.

Immediately below the Chevin, and straddling the River Wharfe, is the little market town of Otley. It has got riverside strolls and rowing boats for hire. Thomas Chippendale, the famous furniture maker, was born in the Manor House in 1718. He didn't just made superb furniture, though; when times were hard he could turn his hand to uPVC windows and loft conversions.

There have been markets in Otley for a thousand years, and the cobbled square – and covered Butter Market – is still the hub of the town. On market days – Fridays and Saturdays – the stalls overflow the square, and line both sides of Kirkgate. The Otley Folk Festival takes place in September. Over a long weekend you can hardly move for mummers and Morris dancers: bearded men who, at a pinch, could get by on just the one passport photo. Maybe Harold Shipman's photo. Otley Show, established in 1796, is the oldest agricultural show in Yorkshire. And there are more pubs and fish-and-chip shops per head of population than any other town I can think of. What greater recommendation could there be?

The link path followed the Chevin ridge, past old, worked-out quarries before dropping down onto Yorkgate, a section of an old road to York. 'Gate' means 'street'; you knew that already. But you may be surprised by what you see next. Passing motorists do a double-take and rub their eyes, for here, grazing contentedly in a small field, is a flock of llamas. Yes, in a quiet corner of West Yorkshire, a llama farmer is plying his esoteric trade.

The path continued through the car-park of the Chevin, a typical, smoke-blackened, West Yorkshire pub. I crossed a railway track – the branch-line from Leeds to the terminus in Ilkley – and into Menston. Passing the railway station, I walked through quiet streets where commuters live, to join a stony track. Amongst fields and copses once again, I passed the farmyard – nay, junkyard – of Hag Farm, up to Burley Woodhead. There's a pub here called The Hermit. If you think there's got to be a story behind a name like that, then you would be right.

The inn sign – showing a tramp-like figure squatting in a cave – commemorates Job Senior. Born in the 1780s, he brought a little colour and notoriety to the village of Burley Woodhead. He worked as a farm labourer; then, unlucky in love, he succumbed to the demon drink.

Job built himself a tiny hovel on the edge of Rombalds Moor. Here he lived on a diet of home-grown potatoes, which he roasted over a peat fire. He cut a strange figure, with a coat of multi-coloured patches, and trousers held up with twine, as he made slow, rheumatic progress around Rombalds Moor with the aid of two crooked sticks. He had long, lank hair, a matted beard and his legs were bandaged with straw. Now there's a man whose fashion sense I can identify with.

Job's eccentric lifestyle soon had people flocking to see him. Of course, people were more easily amused in those days. He offered weather predictions, and advised visitors about their love lives. The possessor of a remarkable voice, he 'sang for his supper' as he lay on his bed of dried bracken and heather. These impromptu performances encouraged Job to sing in nearby villages; he was even welcomed into the theatres of Leeds and Bradford. His speciality was sacred songs, which he would deliver with great feeling. Nevertheless, his unwashed appearance meant that he had to bed down in barns or out-houses. It was while staying in such a barn that he was struck down, aged seventy-seven, with cholera. Job Senior may have died in the workhouse, but his funeral attracted a big crowd.

From the little green at Burley Woodhead, the path climbed through bracken and heather onto Rombalds Moor, with views down over Burley in Wharfedale. According to legend, Rombald was a giant who used to live on these moors. Giants such as Rombald and Wade – and the Devil himself – were busy all over Yorkshire, dropping stones and creating big holes in the ground. It was obviously a way of accounting for some of the more unusual features of the landscape – of which Rombalds Moor has more than its fair share.

But let's stop calling it Rombalds Moor, even though that's how the map has it. To everybody else it's Ilkley Moor, probably the most celebrated stretch of moorland in the land. It's a long ridge of mill-stone grit, immediately to the south of Ilkley: a place of myth, legend, sheep and a fascinating collection of ancient relics. The Twelve Apostles, a ring of Bronze Age standing stones, lie close to the meet-ing of two ancient routes across the moor. But they are merely the most visible evidence of 7000 years of occupation. There are other, smaller circles too, and Ilkley Moor is celebrated for its rock carvings, many featuring 'cup and ring' designs. On the most famous of these rocks is a sinuous swastika: actually a symbol of good luck until the Nazis corrupted it.

Ilkley Moor has always been a great place to walk. For the millhands of Leeds and Bradford, Ilkley Moor represented a day out in the country. It was a proper day out, not just a stroll around a formal park under the reproachful gaze – literally or figuratively – of some mill-owning patrician. The classic ramble has traditionally been straight across the moor to Ilkley, and back the same way. Generations of ramblers have stopped for ham and eggs at Dick Hudson's (actually The Fleece Inn, but always known as Dick Hudson's, after a popular landlord of Queen Victoria's day). It may have been one such ramble, perhaps undertaken by a chapel choir, that inspired the famous song.

'On Ilkley Moor Baht 'At' is a doleful dirge. It sounds cheerful enough – courting Mary Jane, and all that – but only until you take a look at the rest of the verses. Yorkshire folk can take no credit for adopting an unofficial 'national anthem' that flags up such unpalatable truths about the food chain and focuses so morbidly on the inevitability of death. A note for soft Southern bed-wetters: 'On Ilkley Moor Baht 'At' just means 'On Ilkley Moor without a hat on.' At the time the song was written (probably during the latter years of the nineteenth century), walking without a hat was regarded as a sure sign of moral degeneracy.

I came to a farm called York View. On that mythically clear day I'm told you can see York Minster from here. The path hugged the moorland edge, on the level except when I scrambled down to cross Coldstone Beck. I was sauntering happily along, humming songs from *South Pacific*, when a red grouse flew up from under my feet, with heart-stopping suddenness, its call a mocking 'Go back! go back!' I wondered how long it must have taken grouse to learn this simple diversionary tactic, designed to disorientate a shotgun-toting fool into shooting his own foot rather than a plump game-bird.

I soon passed the biggest and best known of Ilkley Moor's rocks, the Cow and Calf. They were created, apparently, by that clumsy giant, Rombald, who dislodged stones from a gritstone outcrop. I've read that the Calf weighs 1000 tons: one of those statistics that seems to ask more questions than it answers. These rocks used to be a complete family unit, until the rock known as the Bull was broken up to provide building stone.

Local climbers come to the rocks to practise their toe-holds and rope-work, and decide whether to break their necks here or somewhere a little more exotic. I stopped to watch one young guy make fitful progress up a precipitous rock-face. Just as I was wondering what would happen to him if he fell off, he fell off. The rope took the strain, thankfully, leaving him dangling upside down, a few feet from the ground, like a marionette in spasm. Climbing: maybe it's a 'women and horses' kind of deal, just one more thing I don't understand.

In evening sunshine I picked my way between the rocks and bracken, passing a building known as White Wells. It was built, in 1700, around a mineral water spring that had long been recognised for its invigorating properties. A century later a pair of plunge-baths were added, where visitors and locals alike could enjoy the masochistic pleasures of bathing in cold water. More of this tomorrow; as I walked down Cowpasture Road into the spa town of Ilkley, I was more intent on climbing into a *hot* bath.

I had fixed myself up with a guesthouse a few days earlier – reckoning that if I couldn't walk from Leeds to Ilkley in a day, then I might as well pack up any idea of finishing the Dales Way. The bath was as good as I'd imagined, and so were the fish and chips I ate about an hour later.

Day Two

ILKLEY TO APPLETREEWICK

Bolton Abbey

T
he next morning, Saturday, I limped down through Ilkley, feeling a bit stiff. The 16 miles I did yesterday hardly consti-tuted a major trek, of course, but then I don't generally follow a day's walking by doing much the same thing all over again. Punishing sessions of isometric inertia have done nothing for my fitness levels.

Unlike me, Ilkley was looking clean, prosperous and rather pleased with itself: hardly surprising since the town is unashamedly dedicat-ed to the good things in life. People who live in, say, Cheltenham or Bath, would feel very much at home in Ilkley, a town that seems to have more in common with Harrogate, its even posher neighbour, than with the rough and ready textile towns of West Yorkshire. Even as late in the year as October, flowers in neat beds spelled out colourful civic slogans: 'No blacks, no Irish.' No, just kidding. But I did see a man clean up his dog's shit with a clean handkerchief and then put it back in his pocket: commendable, I'm sure, but I wouldn't like to work at the place where he takes his dry-cleaning.

The women of Ilkley are sleek and well-groomed. They don't shuffle along the pavement in carpet slippers and house-coats, pushing tartan shopping trolleys and talking to themselves. The women of Ilkley flounce in and out of smart designer shops, clutching smart designer bags, before climbing decorously into some hot little hatchback.

The Romans knew Ilkley as Olicana, an important camp on the way from one God-forsaken outpost of their empire to another. It's only a wild surmise, but I doubt that your average Roman foot-soldier regarded the North of England as a plum posting. He would have been swapping warm weather, a relaxed lifestyle and weekend orgies for thermal underwear, hostile natives and incessant rain. Perhaps it was a punishment for bad behaviour: what a long weekend in Skegness would be for us today.

Once the Romans had left, chastened by the British experience, the locals reverted to type – forgetting just about everything the Romans had taught them. It took many communities a thousand years to create a society as well-ordered as the one the Romans abandoned, with such haste, in AD407. The centre of Ilkley was the centre of Olicana too; the present church lies inside the boundaries of the Roman camp. With the aid of a map (and, it must be said, a fertile imagination) you can trace the rough outline of the camp. Behind the handsome Manor House Museum is a short stretch of original Roman wall.

Until the middle of the nineteenth century, Ilkley was a mere village: 'dirty and insignificant', according to a writer of the time. As with Harrogate, Ilkley's fortunes changed dramatically with the discovery of mineral springs. It was confidently assumed, by ambitious quacks and the idle rich alike, that such foul-tasting water must have medicinal properties. It did a lot of good – especially to entrepreneurial men such as Dr William Macleod. He arrived here in 1847, immediately recognised the town's potential and spent the next twenty-five years creating a place where well-heeled hypochondriacs could 'take the waters' in convivially upmarket surroundings.

During the reign of Queen Victoria, the great and the good came here to socialise at the town's hotels and hydros (precursors of today's health farms). Dr Macleod vigorously promoted the 'Ilkley Cure': a strict regime of exercise and cold baths. He chided the medical profession of his day, recommending only three physicians: 'Air, water and diet'. Good clean air from Ilkley Moor was pumped into Dr Macleod's Compressed Air Bath, at 7½ lbs per square inch above atmospheric pressure: an invigorating procedure, apparently. The diet in his hydropathatic institution, Ben Rhydding, was reckoned to be 'abundant'. And water, in one form or another, was on tap to cure his patients of whatever it was that ailed them.

Water was administered in many forms. Dr Macleod took his magic sponge to aches and pains: a form of treatment now only seen on the football field. Patients were subjected to cold showers and probing douches; they were 'mummified' by being wrapped in wet sheets. The elderly and infirm were treated in vapour baths and steam rooms, where they were pummelled back to a semblance of good health.

We're more sophisticated now, thank goodness, realising that quackery such as the cold water cure belongs to the past. And I said as much to my past-life regressionist, just the other day.

With its open-air swimming pool and riverside promenades, Ilkley was almost an inland resort. Visitor numbers increased with the coming of the railway. Madame Tussaud spent time here. Maybe it was seeing so many comatose people in bathchairs that gave her the idea that would bring her fame and fortune. Charles Darwin took a well-earned rest in Ilkley, before returning to face the furore his book, The Origin of Species, was to cause in the scientific community when it was published in 1859. However, he had more faith in natural selection than in the hydro's cold water cure and went home with more than he came with – complaining about 'a frightful succession of boils'.

It being October, Ilkley's shops were full of masks, bats, witches and other such Hallowe'en junk. Our religious leaders must be kicking themselves for failing to exploit this marketing opportunity. Yes, if only the Church of England could harness some of this Satanic energy, imagine what that could do to church attendances.

Who the hell needs Hallowe'en anyway? It's just one more crap import from the good old US of A, to add to an undistinguished list that includes McDonald's, Coca Cola, Starbucks and Father's Day. One Ilkley grocer was selling pumpkins that were already hollowed out, and carved with a mouth, nose and eyes. At the risk of being a killjoy, doesn't this undermine the admittedly small amount of fun that can be derived from owning an oversized pomegranate?

I made my way down to the three arches of the handsome old bridge – dating back to the 1670s but now closed to all traffic more substantial than a rather overweight man with a pack on his back. A signpost confirmed that this was the official start of the Dales Way. 'Windermere 73 miles,' it read (though the latest *Dales Way Handbook* suggests 84; there's inflation for you). I waited a few minutes on the bridge, hoping another Dales Wayfarer would suddenly appear: a congenial (though mildly eccentric) walking companion with whom I could have had a series of amusingly wacky adventures on the way. I waited some more, drumming my fingers on the old stonework, before hoisting the rucksack onto my back and setting off along the riverside path – on my own. For the first time – but not the last – I wondered about the wisdom of tackling the Dales Way in October.

No matter. The River Wharfe itself is a splendid walking companion: transcendentally still one minute, rushing giddily over rocks and weirs a few seconds later. And, unlike other walking companions, it doesn't witter on and on about high-yield, low-risk saving schemes or the wisdom of buying some new car with airbags, ABS and a whiplash protection system. The River Wharfe doesn't borrow money off you and neglect to pay it back. The Wharfe doesn't make rash promises that subsequently turn to ashes. And, best of all, it doesn't pat you on the stomach (like one or two people of my acquaintance; they know who they are) with the fatuous observation that 'You've put on a pound or two.'

The Wharfe is also a pleasant change from the river that runs through my home town of Hebden Bridge. There are no ripples in the Calder; a light breeze just makes it wobble, like grey jelly. If the water was any more polluted, you'd be able to cut it into slices. Drop a match in and the whole damn river might blow. If you ever see a fish jump, it will only be to catch its breath. The tumbling waters of the Wharfe were used to power a few mills, but the river never suffered the indignities heaped on, say, the Calder and the Aire. The watercourses of industrial West Yorkshire had to absorb as many dyestuffs and noxious chemicals as was compatible with the rivers remaining in a more or less liquid state.

Within a few minutes of leaving Ilkley I had seen the first of many dippers. And a grey heron, motionless in the shallows, its head hunched into its shoulders. Surrounded by a garrulous bunch of mallards, the heron had a pained expression – like an old guy whose peace and quiet is interrupted by noisy kids. Then, best of all, I glimpsed the metallic blue flash of a kingfisher.

I'm a big fan of dippers. They're specialists; they know exactly where they want to live. They don't cast envious glances at brochures for time-share apartments on the Costa Blanca; no, all they ask from life is a fast-flowing beck in upland country. You won't see dippers anywhere else. They can't bear to be away from water, even for a second; when they take to the wing it's only to fly up-river or down. They're not interested in what goes on beyond the river bank. If there's a bridge over the beck, dippers will fly under, never over. That's the kind of pull that water has on dippers.

They pose on rocks in the water – plump little black birds, with a starched white breast – doing the little curtseys from which they get their name. But they're not just a comic turn; they can perform a trick that's unique among British birds. Dippers, bless 'em, can walk underwater.

The Dales Way path was well-waymarked at this early stage, to a surreal degree. Whenever the route made even the slightest deviation – to circumnavigate a pile of dog shit, say – a sign offered guidance and reassurance. It was ironic, because the path itself was impossible to lose; all I had to do was keep the river to my right.

Low Mill, built close to the river in 1789, is reckoned to have been the first successful worsted mill in the world. That's successful in the sense that the worsted yarn was spun by machine. The first consignment of machine-spun wool from Low Mill was the cause of amazement in Bradford; it was this trade that would subsequently make the city's fortune. Low Mill was the scene of a Luddite riot in the early years of the nineteenth century. Shearers and croppers feared that the new-fangled machines would destroy their livelihoods (they were right, of course), so they attacked the mills where the machines were being installed.

Luddites have had a bad press over the years, becoming a byword for backwards-looking intransigence. You're a Luddite if you can't programme a VCR to record the football while you're down the pub. You're a Luddite if you don't spend your leisure hours downloading porn from the internet. You're a Luddite if you think there's still a place for paper, pens, books and other outdated nonsense.

Yes, at a time when mill owners held the whip hand (often in the most literal sense), the Luddites talked a lot of sense. Count me in.

Out of the ruins of Low Mill, a small community has sprung up. Low Mill Village tries to look as though it wasn't built five minutes ago. It looks a very pleasant place to set up home – offering river views and a reassuringly Luddite-free lifestyle.

Having crossed the tiniest packhorse bridge I've ever seen, by the Old Rectory, I passed Addingham church into Addingham itself. Now that it has been by-passed by the A65, this little town has the unhurried air of a Dales community. But many of the buildings are three storeys high – with a room under the eaves to house a hand-weaving loom. In addition to Low Mill, the town once boasted no fewer than five textile mills. You could say, with some justification, that Addingham is where industrial West Yorkshire ends and rural North Yorkshire begins.

This isn't one of those compact Yorkshire villages that huddles around a village green. The houses of Addingham straggle for more than a mile along both sides of the main street. So it's no surprise that the village used to be known as Long Addingham, and that it is actually an amalgamation of three separate villages that expanded along with the textile trades.

I popped into a pub, for a pint and a pie. By an amazing coincidence, Manchester United were playing Leeds United at that very moment, and the match was showing on Sky. It was an early kick-off, to encourage the fans to fight each other stone-cold sober. I cast my eyes over the pump clips on the bar, in search of a decent beer. The allegiance of the true football fan, fuelled by envy and hatred of the Red Devils, can be summed up as 'anyone but United'. These days I feel much the same about beer; for me it's 'anything but Tetleys'.

Instead of the cold, tasteless, heavily advertised Creamflow nonsense it is now, Tetley's used to be a wonderful pint. Hard to believe, I know, but it was. Before the company embarked on a strategy of global domination, it concentrated on its 'core activity': fermenting yeast, hops, malt and barley in the correct proportions to produce a session bitter to be proud of. It's a pretty serviceable rule of thumb: the amount of money spent advertising a beer is in inverse proportion to its quality. Which says all you need to know about the brewery's output today.

When I used to live in Leeds, beer was Tetley's. You didn't order a pint of Tetley's; you ordered 'a pint', and what you got was Tetley's. No problem with that. A pint of Tetley's, in a traditional 'sleever' glass (a piece of perfect design, to my eye), was something to treasure. Creamflow was still many years off, but there was just enough Watney's Red Barrel – bright, fizzy beer of stunning blandness – to suggest what the future would hold.

Pouring a pint of Tetley's was quite a performance – not just a matter of flicking a switch. It was hand-pulled: always a recommendation, no matter what the context. And with the beer being drawn up by handpump, barmaids needed well-developed biceps. Nor was the great god Hygiene worshipped with as much blind faith as it is today. Thank goodness. The beer was pulled up to the top of the glass, and beyond. It cascaded down the side of the glass and over the barmaid's forearm in an arresting display of fluvial eroticism. On and on: maybe two pints-worth to overfill the glass and create the creamy head that Yorkshire drinkers prefer. And the beer that over-flowed was decanted into a huge drip tray, before (we assumed) taking a serpentine route back into the cellar, to begin the long journey into the next drinker's glass.

The public health people eventually outlawed this simple practice, even though it was a crime without a victim. No drinker ever complained that his beer had been cascading down a barmaid's arm. Quite the opposite; it was the high point of many a night out. Instead of gunning for easy targets and upsetting blameless Tetley's drinkers, the inspectors could have been doing something more useful. Like persuading the staff in restaurant kitchens to stop gobbing in the food; it's not enough just to make them gargle with Listerene first.

A worse crime has been committed since those heady days. As the brewers have signally failed to find the holy grail – a canned beer that tastes like draught beer (it tastes of *can*, guys) – they have made the imaginative leap of trying to make draught beer taste like canned beer. And with the introduction of Tetley's Creamflow, this bizarre ambition has finally been achieved. Cheers.

Manchester United vs Leeds United was a fixture that brought back some uncomfortable memories. Then, as now, it was just about the biggest game of the season. If you were feeling magnanimous, you would say the fans were passionate; if you weren't, you would call them nutters. Years ago I went to Elland Road with a mate to watch Leeds play Man U. Gordon and I were nominally Leeds fans, but had no scarves or over-priced replica shirts to identify us. In a crowded confusion we were herded into the visitors' end.

Once we'd realised the error, there was no way to get out. If we had tried to catch the stewards' attention ('Help, help... There's been a mistake. We're Leeds fans, but you've locked us in a with a load of big, scary guys with red scarves and tattoos on their knuckles. Let us out...'), we would only have been identified – weeks later – by our dental records. The game proved to be the most uncomfortable ninety minutes I've ever experienced (with my clothes on, anyway).

It wasn't the time or the place for misplaced heroics, and our allegiances weren't seriously tested. We cheered Manchester United to the echo, of course we did, and bit our lips when the home team scored. After the final whistle, an announcement came over the Tannoy, telling Manchester fans to stay in their section until the Leeds fans had dispersed. The Leeds fans had an announcement of their own. Their voices were raised in a note-perfect rendition, in 40,000-part harmony, of that lovely old spiritual, 'We're gonna fuckin' kill ya.' Holding the Manchester fans back merely allowed the Leeds fans to regroup outside the ground and tool themselves up for a few hours of Old Testament retribution.

I looked at Gordon and he looked at me. Having survived the game itself with our good looks intact, it seemed we were now going to be beaten to a bloody pulp by fellow Leeds fans: a fate of almost Shakespearean irony and pathos. We left the ground in a tight scrum of Man U fans, who seemed in no way fazed by being outnumbered by, oh, maybe fifty to one. We swaggered down the road, a veritable tsunami of red rage (a tsunami, incidentally, is a tidal wave... not to be confused with the Toon Army, which is a collection of Newcastle United fans). As we passed a house with a handsome hedge, I looked at Gordon, he looked at me and we dived over the hedge onto somebody's front lawn. We practised, *sotto voce*, the difficult middle eight of 'We're gonna fuckin' kill ya,' until the immediate danger had passed, before re-emerging a few minutes later as fully paid-up Leeds fans.

Years later I now joined the men-only scrum around the bar of a pub in Addingham, to watch a red-faced Roy Keane – a man who earns more in a week than I earn in a year – scream profanities into the referee's face from a distance of about six inches. The beautiful game? I don't think so...

I actually like football. It's not a proper game, like cricket, but it's something to watch in a pub when the conversation is flagging. What I most enjoy, though, is a good game. I don't much care who wins, though this is something I generally keep to myself. At various times in the past I've tried – but always failed – to care about one team or another. I feel silly and self-conscious if I cheer for something as amorphous as 'football'. So I try to join in the banter: wondering what the goalie keeps in that little bag of his, or, since there's safety in numbers, why it is that managers never decide to take *two* games at a time? I award style points for a penalty-winning dive inside the box. I can rhapsodise, with the rest of the guys, about the sheer poetry of a cynical, career-threatening, two-footed tackle from behind.

Everyone in the bar seemed to support Leeds, so I cheered for Leeds too. I've learned my lesson the hard way: there was no point getting beaten up by irate Leeds fans at such an early stage in the walk. In any case, I still have a soft spot for the club. A girlfriend from years ago was rumoured to have lost her virginity at a Leeds United home game. I had assumed it was nothing more than idle gossip. But it may have explained why she could never really relax, sexually speaking, unless the bedroom was full of cheering fans. On small incompatibilities such as this can relationships falter.

There was a good atmosphere in the pub. The young lads were winding up one of the old geezers. 'I'll explain the offside rule just one more time to you fellows,' he said wearily, as they exchanged conspiratorial winks. I drained my pint and hoisted the rucksack over my shoulders. The match score? I can't remember, but, in a very real sense, I believe that football was the winner.

I left Addingham, with the path continuing to hug the river bank. As I walked through a caravan park, a sign indicated that the private beach was for the sole use of caravanners. This 'beach' was a patch of grey sand no bigger than a picnic blanket. Marvellous. With amenities like this on offer, why would anyone even *think* of going abroad for their holidays?

I met a farmer at about the only point in the day when I wasn't quite sure which way to go. I gave him the traditional sheep farmer's greeting, 'Tup of the morning,' and asked him where the Dales Way had gone. 'A lot of walkers go the wrong way here,' he smirked. 'Well, wouldn't it help if you put up a little sign?' I said, with a voice of sweet reason. 'Then people wouldn't get lost, they'd keep to the path and they wouldn't need to bother you by asking the way.' He looked at me as if I was trying to deny him his one pleasure in life.

Why are some farmers so hostile to walkers? Is it simple envy: that farmers work while walkers play? Some ramblers have a bad attitude, of course they do: leaving gates open, dropping litter and disturbing livestock. But I can't believe there are many, compared to the number who are strenuously law-abiding and who regard the country code as being written on tablets of stone. For myself, I take endless pains to keep to recognised rights of way, for a variety of reasons. I don't want to come up against an impassable obstacle. I don't want to get lost. I don't want to upset farmers. And if I ever bother a busy farmer, it will only to be to confirm that I'm on the right track or, if I'm not, so he can point me in the right direction.

The Right to Roam legislation is making farmers twitchy. To hear them talk, you would imagine that hordes of rampaging ramblers were going to lay waste to the farmers' land, in a frenzied re-run of the Harrying of the North. It's mildly intriguing to hear, from certain landowners and farmers, that you (yes, mild-mannered *you*...) are a member of a group that is doing untold damage to the countryside. Of all the problems that hill farmers face (and that's a hell of a lot right now), woolly-hatted ramblers would seem to be among the more benign. And even the most anti-social walker is a mere beginner, a harmless dilettante, compared to the professional desecrators of our countryside.

A number of companies have the right to quarry limestone within the Yorkshire Dales National Park. It makes good roadstone, apparently. Yes, that's right, we are digging up the Dales to create more roads: a pioneering example of selling off the family silver. These quarrying licences date back many years – before the Dales had National Park status – and some of them will remain in force for many years to come. Barring some kind of miracle, those who love the Yorkshire Dales will have to sit on their hands, bite their lips and put up with this institutionalised vandalism for a while longer. What a shambles.

There's the Ministry of Defence, too. Near Leyburn, in Wensleydale, whole tracts of moorland are sealed off from walkers and other undesirables, for the purpose of target practice and tank training. The MoD doesn't bother with fences or razor wire to keep the riff-raff out; a few signs are all it takes: 'DANGER. MILITARY TARGET AREA. DO NOT TOUCH ANYTHING. IT MAY EXPLODE AND KILL YOU.' Well, these signs certainly have the required effect on me.

Let's not forget the developers who won't be content until every field has been transformed into a golf course, and every valley into a time-share holiday complex. And they've no sense of shame about what they're doing. Whenever they're accused of raping the countryside, they trot out those same tired excuses. Not only do they deny raping the countryside, they insist that the countryside 'dressed provocatively' and was 'leading them on'.

Then there are the khaki-clad 4x4 boys. Having bought an off-road vehicle nearly as big as one of the MoD's tanks, with bull-bars, big knobbly tyres and all the aerodynamic qualities of a breeze-block, these doylems spend their weekends churning up green lanes into knee-deep mud. Let's not forget the farmers themselves; there are one or two who would rip their grandmother's throat open with a billhook if that would guarantee another EEC subsidy cheque. And then you have the country landowners who feel they can keep great swathes of moorland to themselves, just because their ancestors licked William the Conqueror's arse to most timely effect after the Norman invasion. Oh, don't get me started...

A couple of miles out of Addingham, beyond Bolton Bridge, there was a sign. Embossed with the curly-horned head of a Swaledale ram, it announced that I was now entering the Yorkshire Dales National Park. Real countryside, at last. Hooray. Though dales can be found throughout the North of England – from the Peak District to the North Pennines, from the North York Moors in the east to the Lake District in the west – the Dales of Yorkshire are definitive. You can even miss out the word 'Yorkshire'; 'The Dales' will suffice.

In a move that was largely welcomed, the Yorkshire Dales National Park was created in 1954. Less happily, the Local Government Act of 1972 consigned the North, West and East ridings of Yorkshire to the dustbin of history. What a nerve. The ridings (from the Old Norse, meaning 'a third part'; but you knew that already) probably date back as far as the ninth century, when much of the North of England was under Danish rule. Perhaps Yorkshire came off lightly from the boundary changes; at least it still exists. The good people of Rutland woke up one morning – April Fool's Day, 1974, it was – to find their county wiped clean off the map.

To the bureaucratic mind, preferring bland uniformity to mild idiosyncrasy, Yorkshire's boundaries must have seemed unnecessarily eccentric. Never mind that the ridings had existed for more than a thousand years. Never mind that they were understood by all. They were seen as quaint anachronisms. They had to go.

Once the civil servants had jettisoned the ridings, it was 'open season' on other aspects of Yorkshire identity too. The boundaries of the county have stretched and contracted over the years, like a length of knicker elastic. Whenever things have been a bit slack in local government offices, faceless bureaucrats have taken time off from their busy schedules (making chains of paper clips and gazing out of the window) to take increasingly bizarre decisions about exactly what – and where – Yorkshire is.

Middlesbrough and Darlington were summarily slung out; no great loss, some might say. The Forest of Bowland has been passed on to Lancashire, which is Lancashire's gain. The little town of Dent, with its cobbled streets and whitewashed cottages, used to be in West Yorkshire. Now, bizarrely, it contrives to be both in the Yorkshire Dales National Park and in Cumbria. Tan Hill Inn seems to slip from North Yorkshire to County Durham and back again on a regular basis – as though life wasn't eccentric enough already at England's highest and most isolated pub. And Humberside: what the hell was *that* all about?

Had I tackled the Dales Way before 1974, I could have walked for five whole days – as far as Sedbergh, in fact – without leaving the West Riding of Yorkshire. In Lower Wharfedale the boundary between North and West Yorkshire now follows the meandering course of the Wharfe. Maybe none of this matters – a rose by any other name, and all that – but it matters to me.

As I entered the National Park, the sun came out. I took it as a good omen. I held a kissing gate open for a couple of elderly ladies, who asked me where I was going. 'We've done the Dales Way,' said one. 'Both ways,' said the other. 'Twice,' they said in unison, putting me firmly in my place before striding off together.

The next sign confirmed that I was now entering the Duke of Devonshire's estate. Isn't it typical of our convoluted class system, that the Duke of Devonshire, of all places, should own a chunk of Yorkshire? 'Keep strictly to the waymarked footpath through the estate,' the sign read. 'We maintain this so-called right-of-way under protest, and begrudge every second that you are on our land.' No, not really.

You never know, though. The Duke of Devonshire once wrote a letter to the National Park Authority, with the aim of safeguarding his grouse-shooting interests. This was his reason for wanting to exclude the public from his land for even more days each year:

'Sound management dictates that these birds are shot, otherwise they will succumb to fatal diseases...' It's good to know that the welfare of our game birds is in such good hands. Yes, we don't want grouse and partridges catching fatal diseases, when they could be blasted out of the sky instead by parties of Japanese businessmen. Heaven forbid.

And how about this as a reason for keeping walkers out of woodland?

It's common knowledge that trees need privacy to grow to their full height. If they so much as hear the tramping of ramblers' boots, some trees have been known to abort their seedlings. It's vital that these woods remain undisturbed, and in responsible private ownership.

I think I made that up, but I'm not 100 per cent sure. Country landowners are busy updating the Country Code. They're taking out the dead wood – all that guff about making sure you shut gates and taking litter home – thus reducing the code to this simple, easily remembered injunction:

Is your visit to our land really necessary?
It's not, is it?
So bugger off smartish, before I set the dogs on you.

On a sunny Saturday Bolton Abbey was predictably awash with visitors. Elbowing my way through the crowds it was easy to believe the figures, generally held by those whose task it is to manage tourism in our beauty spots, that 80 per cent of visitors go to just 20 per cent of the places. A trip to Bolton Abbey is a day out in the way that, say, a trip to Keighley palpably isn't. Bolton Abbey has lazy riverside walks, genuine history and evocative ruins that inspired no less a painter than JMW Turner to enshrine them on canvas. Bolton Abbey is the epitome of the picturesque, attracting poets such as William Wordsworth and John Ruskin to sing its praises. Keighley, on the other hand, is where you'd go if you wanted to establish an unshakeable alibi, or buy a gross of suppositories, or perhaps be tested, discreetly, for some sexually transmitted disease.

The monks of some monastic orders used to choose the most inhospitable places to build their monasteries, hoping that a combination of bleak terrain, cold baths, self-flagellation and baleful silence would bring them ever closer to a savage and vengeful God. But when Bolton Abbey was built here, in 1154, on a bend in the river, it must surely have been on aesthetic grounds. The monks of Bolton Abbey belonged to the Augustinian order and took vows of obedience and chastity, but, revealingly, not poverty. To judge from the few account books that have survived, the monks lived well and entertained handsomely, putting away prodigious quantities of food and wine. It makes roly-poly Friar Tuck seem less of a caricature and more like a study from life.

The monks of Bolton and other abbeys (as far afield as Furness Abbey in Cumbria, and Kirkstall Abbey in Leeds) became major landowners in the Dales. They established outlying farms – known as granges – where they kept livestock (mostly sheep and cattle), bred horses, traded in wool and mined for lead and iron ore. In the process they created work for a large labour force of lay brothers and local people. The good life came to a sudden and inglorious end in 1539 when, on the orders of King Henry VIII, this community was disbanded. The nave of the old priory was saved from destruction, however, and now serves as the village's parish church.

Cows graze contentedly in the pasture beneath the abbey ruins; couples canoodle; kids play safely on a sandy beach by the river. It really is a most beautiful spot. A note for pedants: the ruin is actually of Bolton *Priory*; Bolton Abbey is the little village that grew up around it. The village now consists of a few picturesque cottages and a handsome tithe barn – all dwarfed by a car park the size of the Isle of Man. Oh, and a station on the recently extended Embsay Steam Railway, for enthusiasts of very short train journeys.

Having crossed the river on a wooden footbridge, I passed a fallen tree. Thousands of coins had been hammered into its trunk over the years. It was a surreal sight, like an illustration from a Mervyn Peake novel. The next couple of miles illustrated both the best and the worst aspects of the Yorkshire Dales. The riverside path was a delight. But the overflowing car park at Cavendish Pavilion reaffirmed the bizarre fact that people are happy to drive 'up the Dales' and pay good money to park their cars in regimented rows, before spending an hour or two, with the windows up, drinking milky tea from a Thermos flask or, just to liven things up, sucking a boiled sweet from the tin in the glove compartment. This is merely a preamble for the main event of the day: reading the Sunday papers from cover to cover. If you ever see me doing that, please put me out of my misery with a well-aimed bullet. It would be a kindness.

Recrossing the river on another wooden bridge, I hurried past the pavilion itself, which is a large and popular cafe. The good weather was encouraging people to sit outside: mountain bikers in skin-tight, day-glo Lycra, and couples in matching cagoules and suspiciously clean walking boots.

The high point of day two was walking through Bolton Woods. In afternoon sunshine, the autumn tints were at their very best. My nostrils were assailed by those evocative autumn smells of pepper, liquorice and macaroons. Designated a Site of Special Scientific Interest, the woods are a naturalists' paradise. Those who love mosses and liverworts with unbridled passion will not be disappointed.

These are some of the finest deciduous woods in the National Park. That's not such a great boast because if there's one kind of habitat that's under-represented in the Dales, it's old broadleaved woodland. There are plenty of conifer plantations, though. Conifers grow fast, and no doubt constitute a profitable cash crop. But they are boring to walk through: filled with gloom and silence and almost totally devoid of wildlife. Give me a shady oak wood any day.

As with so many other features of our countryside, Bolton Woods are not quite as natural as they first appear. The paths were laid out, during the nineteenth century, by a local vicar who had an eye for the picturesque. Walkers can now choose between high-level and riverside routes, beneath the canopies of sycamore, beech and oak trees. I took the low road, so I could check out the famous Strid, a narrow, rocky gorge which constricts the river's flow into an impressive torrent. You would need to be a fool – or the Boy Egremond – even to think of jumping across the river at this point. It's not that the distance is so great, more that the rocks are slippery – especially when the river is in spate. One little slip and you could end up like the Boy Egremond: swept away and never seen again.

The Boy Egremond made his fateful leap more than 700 years ago. Why did he attempt it? We'll never know. But being known as the Boy Egremond ('I'm almost a *man*, mother') probably had something to do with it. He was out hunting one day, with his faithful greyhound at his side. When he tried to leap across the Strid, the hound stood its ground. The leash tightened, the Boy Egremond lost his footing and he vanished... sucked fatally into the river's fierce undertow. The Strid, you see, may only be a few feet wide, but it's very deep. The gritstone rock has been worn away by swirling water into caves and hollows. So don't even think about jumping.

As I scuffed my boots through the fallen leaves in Bolton Woods, I consulted my list of bed and breakfast establishments and, a mite self-consciously, tapped a number into my smart new mobile phone. All I got out of it, though, were a few unhelpful bleeps. I cursed Mr Branson, and my own gullibility, for buying a phone that wouldn't work 'up the Dales'. I prayed that the bearded loon would launch a balloon just one more time, and attempt the last great adventure: setting a compass bearing right into the heart of the sun. I hurled the phone back into my rucksack and crossed the river again, on an aqueduct built to carry water from the reservoirs in Nidderdale to the thirsty mill towns of West Yorkshire. The Dales Way now hugged the eastern bank of the Wharfe. Barden Bridge was next: with its three arches and massive buttresses, it was almost a carbon copy of the old bridge at Ilkley.

Close by is Barden Tower, a hunting lodge that once belonged to Lady Anne Clifford: a redoubtable lady who left her mark indelibly on the northern counties. Her father, the 3rd Earl of Cumberland, died in 1605, when she was just fifteen years old. As his only child she should have inherited a number of properties in Yorkshire and Westmorland (including five castles: Skipton, Pendragon, Appleby,

Brough and Brougham) but her father's will favoured her uncle instead. Undaunted, Lady Anne set about righting this wrong. In the process she defied two profligate husbands, the Archbishop of Canterbury and even King James I. It took Anne thirty-eight years of cussed perseverance to win her inheritance, by which time she was a widow twice over, and almost sixty years old.

Lady Anne dedicated the rest of her long life to visiting – and restoring – her properties in the North. She travelled, as befitted a noble lady, in a litter slung between horses, followed by a huge retinue of servants, retainers and hired hands. Whenever she moved, all her household effects went with her: not just a few trinkets, but beds and furniture too. And there were always gifts for her family, friends and tenants. A procession of horses and carriages making painfully slow progress over the high Yorkshire fells: what a remarkable sight that must have been. No wonder she is remembered so fondly today.

In 1658, finding Barden Tower in ruins, she built it up again – marking the occasion, characteristically, with an inscribed stone tablet. She decided to rebuild Skipton Castle, her birthplace, too: a provocative act during the volatile years of the Civil War. Having laid siege to the castle for three long years, Oliver Cromwell's Parliamentarian troops had dismantled the castle's defences, to stop it ever being used again to promote the Royalist cause. When Cromwell heard of her plans to restore Skipton Castle, he was mindful of Lady Anne's reputation. 'Nay, let her build what she will,' he is reported to have said, 'She shall have no hindrance from me.'

After Lady Anne's death, aged eighty-six, all her work was undone. Her will stipulated that the castles and houses should be shared out between her two daughters and one granddaughter. Considering her own long fight to claim her inheritance, Lady Anne would have despaired to see her grandson defy the will and make a successful claim on the estate. He had no need of castles. Though he kept Appleby Castle in good repair, the cad let most of the others fall into ruin once again.

There was more beautiful woodland, and more white water, as I approached the village of Appletreewick, 'the village by the apple trees'. The evening light was beautiful too, bathing the village in a peach-coloured light. Appletreewick is a gorgeous little place, and has a name to match (say 'Aptrick' if you want to sound like a local). The houses straggle along either side of the road, from the top of the hill to the bottom: a linear pattern that's typical of Nordic villages. In medieval times Appletreewick was a place of rather more importance than it is today, one of the outlying granges belonging to the monks of Bolton Priory. One of the village's splendid old houses, Mock Beggar Hall, was formerly known as Monks' Hall. Its architecture is as whimsical as its name.

I booked my bed and breakfast from a call box, and got directions, which I promptly forgot. 'You can't miss it,' I was told, a tad optimistically. Relieved to know I had somewhere to lay my head, my thoughts turned to a pint or two and a plateful of something stodgy enough to stick to a hungry man's ribs. While most villages of similar size have no pub at all, Appletreewick has a choice of two. The New Inn and Craven Arms lie a hundred yards apart, like twins – sharing the valley view but separated by a bend in the road.

I can remember when the New Inn had a unique claim to fame: if there was another no-smoking pub in the land, then I'd never heard of it. At the time – the 1970s – banning smokers from a boozer was unheard-of; in a small Dales village it looked like commercial suicide. It seemed to make no more sense than banning unsightly women or men with beards. But the landlord, John Showers, had seen a close friend of his succumb to lung cancer, and decided to wage a one-man war against the evils of tobacco.

Anyone who had the temerity to wander into his pub with a fag in his mouth was roundly abused and – I've seen it happen – drenched with a well-aimed burst from the soda syphon that sat on the bar. Yes, he was what you might call a bit of a character, that Mr Showers, and didn't he know it. With his cravat, his overbearing manner and his outspoken views, he enjoyed playing the eccentric host. The toilet walls in the gents' toilet (I can't vouch for the ladies) were covered in newspaper clippings about him and his no-smoking pub.

How times have changed. These days his views would be regarded as mainstream. Mr Showers had the courage of his convictions, anticipating a time when smokers would be left – literally or figuratively – out in the cold. There are plans, I hear, to print horrific pictures on cigarette packets – charred lungs, diseased hearts, furred-up arteries, etc – to make smokers feel even worse than they do already. But if a message as unambiguous as 'Tobacco Kills' doesn't make smokers give up, will a forensic photograph make any difference?

A few years ago I saw a picture of a woman who had had a tobacco-related tracheotomy. Despite losing the power of speech, she was still smoking. Except that now (and I hope you're not eating as you read this) she had to inhale the cigarette smoke through a small hole in her neck. A picture of *her* on a fag-packet, enjoying a quiet smoke, might make people think twice about lighting up.

I did my stint as a smoker, happy to hand money over to tobacco companies and help to fill the government coffers. But it wasn't the money that made me stop; one day I just realised that smoking wasn't much fun any more. After one or two false starts I managed to quit the habit, joining the ranks of smug ex-smokers. And, let's face it, people don't come much smugger than that.

Products as dangerous as cigarettes aren't freely available from corner shops, with or without health warnings (Napalm: 'Not for indoor use'? Scud missiles: 'Fire away from body'?). Cigarettes are just too dangerous to be sold at all. One day some government may grasp the nettle: banning cigarettes altogether and treating smokers as the addicts they are, who need a lot of help to kick the habit. Meanwhile, we'll let smokers carry on puffing, as they shorten their breath and their life expectancy. We'll treat them like social pariahs, we'll print horror pictures on their cigarette packets and we'll tax them to the hilt. It's enough to make a smug ex-smoker feel rather sorry for them.

John Showers and his soda syphon are long gone, so I pushed open the door of the Craven Arms instead, for a meal and a couple of beers. The pub commemorates a local family, whose most prominent member was Sir William Craven. Born in Appletreewick, he went to London to seek his fortune, rising from being a humble tailor's apprentice to become, in 1611, Lord Mayor of London. He may have been the inspiration for the story of Dick Whittington.

By the time I left the pub, and started to walk towards the guest-house, it was dark. Not 'city dark,' but 'country dark': no moon in the sky, not a single winking star. A total, enveloping, all-pervading darkness... and me without a torch. I berated myself for not packing one, and cursed Mr Branson again, just for the hell of it. I'd forgotten just how dark the sky is, beyond the reach of street-lights. It's *really* dark...

I walked blindly down the road with my arms stretched out in front of me, like one of the zombies in The Night of the Living Dead. I lost my bearings – bumping into walls and sinking into mud, or worse. Tree branches whipped my face. I heard night birds call and the scraping sounds as a drooling madman sharpened his axe. Why had I blithely assumed that I would be able to find my way in the dark? My sense of direction deserted me; I was thoroughly lost. There was nothing wrong with my imagination, though. Anything seemed possible on a night like this: UFOs, alien abduction, Chelsea buying an English player. Anything except me finding the bloody guesthouse.

Myths and legends survived longer in country areas than they did in the towns. Strange creatures were born of fears and fancies; the darkness was visited by sprites, bogles and hobgoblins. Monsters walked abroad: the werewolf, the vampire and the manticore, a terrifying beast which had the body of a lion and the head of a borough surveyor. There are stories aplenty in Wharfedale – and especially a nearby limestone gorge called, tellingly, Trollers Gill – about a spectral dog called the Barghest, which has blazing red eyes as big as saucers. A guidebook blithely suggests that such stories sound a bit fanciful to our sophisticated twenty-first century sensibilities. Well, I can only say that the writer of that book had never spent an hour wandering around in total darkness, with spooky noises accompanying his every step.

A full hour after I'd left the pub, I stumbled gratefully into the guest-house, babbling words of gratitude to the lady of the house. She showed me all I needed to see: a bed with clean cotton sheets, and electric lights that went on and off with a flick of the switch. On and off, on and off, just like that. On and off. Bliss.

APPLETREEWICK TO KETTLEWELL

Limestone Pavement

Having taken so long to find the guesthouse the previous night, I was loathe to leave it. It was very comfortable: all stripped pine, pastel colours and fluffy towels. On any other day I would have been quite content to plump up the pillows, and spend the morning eating continental chocolates and watching 'Kilroy'. But there was walking to be done. Mine host likened himself to Basil Fawlty, though in truth he and his wife had perfected a polished double act. They provided a full English breakfast in the conservatory, accompanied by toast and faultless one-liners.

The day began brightly, as I rejoined the riverside path. Having changed his mind about slitting my throat from ear to ear, the mad axeman was nowhere to be seen. Maybe we're not as sophisticated as we like to think we are, and the darkness still holds primeval terrors. Or maybe it was just me, being a wimp. Anyway, the landscape that had seemed so oppressive in the night was now wonderfully calm. Mist hung in the valley and a light frost clung to the roofs of the farms and houses. They looked as though they'd been dusted with icing sugar. It seemed as though the earth itself had been freshly minted that very morning. I felt a poem coming on. But no, it was just wind.

I soon approached Burnsall, across its old stone bridge. This is another of the Dales' honey-pot villages, not least because the village green extends to the river bank and children can paddle safely in the shallows. Burnsall was nearly as crowded as Bolton Abbey had been. People unaware of the full horrors of picnicking were laying rugs out on the grass.

From a distance (there are grand views to be had from Burnsall Fell), you can see that this is another typical Dales village. The massive, five-arched bridge spans a broad meander in the river. The church tower rises head and shoulders above a huddle of stone houses, with the fells, criss-crossed by dry stone walls, as a backdrop. What makes Burnsall so enchanting is that the village is 'all of a piece,' with most of the buildings dating from the great period of rebuilding: the second half of the seventeenth century.

Though he made good in London, Sir William Craven never forgot his Wharfedale roots. He paid for the rebuilding of Burnsall Bridge, in 1612, after it had been washed away in a flood. He restored Burnsall church, and its unusual lych-gate, and was the main benefactor in establishing the nearby grammar school. Both buildings are worth a closer look.

I watched two enormous coaches block the road for ten minutes, as they tried to perform an inelegant 23-point turn, before I escaped from the traffic mayhem. I walked between the bridge and the Red Lion Inn, to continue on the riverside path. This is a particularly delightful stretch of river, where the Wharfe rushes through the limestone gorge of Loup Scar. In warmer weather I have seen kids leaping off the rocks here and plunging down into the river. But I don't recommended this foolhardy act any more than trying to leap the Strid... unless you're fifteen and have a pressing need to impress the girls.

Lost in my thoughts I rounded a bend and bumped into Frank, another writer of 'outdoorsy' books. He was taking the opportunity, on a sunny Sunday morning, to take a walk with friends. It was quite a surprise; Frank was the last person I'd expected to meet. I had it on good authority that he'd been had up for performing an unnatural act with a farm animal. Not a sheep (which wouldn't have raised too many eyebrows in the Dales) but an undeniably attractive heifer called Daisy.

There's still a lot of prejudice about a man who forms a loving relationship with another species. Society has many ways of signalling its disapproval: everything from withholding the man's pension rights to firebombing his house. We tend to get very judgemental about such matters – jumping to predictable conclusions – but has anyone asked the animals concerned what they would prefer? A steel bolt through the cranium in a slaughterhouse, or a respectful (and possibly consensual) relationship with a caring man of letters? This sort of inter-species relationship should encourage us not merely to condemn but to ask questions too. Like what happens when the relationship turns sour? Who keeps the milk quota? And who gets custody of the barn?

These were the kind of thoughts that were running through my mind as I tried to make small talk to Frank. I tried – believe me, I tried – to think of a tactful way to frame the obvious question, without embarrassing the poor man in front of his walking companions: 'I know there's never a good time to ask this, Frank, but has that cow-shagging case come to court yet?' Yes, sometimes the straightforward approach is the best.

I crossed the Wharfe once again, on a springy suspension footbridge near Hebden: a nineteenth-century replacement for a line of stepping stones. This is where Hebden Beck – one of the dale's hardest-worked tributaries – drains into the Wharfe. A century and a half ago, the water from Hebden Beck was used to power pumps, crushers and other machinery in the lead mines high up on Grassington Moor. I followed an avenue of chestnut trees by the broad, still river; this approach to Grassington is one of the loveliest sections of the Dales Way.

Like Bolton Abbey, the church of St Michael and All Angels occupies a delightful site on a bend in the river. With its broad, low roof and diminutive bell tower, it fits snugly into the landscape. The solitary position might suggest that the church was a surviving relic of one of Yorkshire's vanished villages. But it was actually built (or, at least, begun) in the twelfth century, to serve a total of four parishes: Grassington, Linton, Hebden and Threshfield. And to avoid any kind of favouritism to one parish over another, the church stands aloof and distant from all four villages. That's fair, isn't it: make it inconvenient for *everyone* to get to church? In compensation, good paths converge on the church from all points of the compass – including stepping stones across the river – which helped churchgoers to arrive dry-shod for their devotions.

I haven't always had a taste for old churches. Until a few years ago I really couldn't give a flying buttress about ecclesiastical architecture. It's an interest that creeps up on you unawares. One minute you're 'getting down' in the disco and 'strutting your funky stuff'. Then, without any warning, you walk into old churches and – with a dreamy, faraway look in your eye – start fondling the woodwork. It's a reliable sign of ageing – up there with visiting garden centres and developing a heightened awareness of Croft Original sherry.

But middle age isn't too painful; you just have to be aware of the signs. Old folk don't flinch any more when they see you approaching; they don't clutch their purses more tightly. 'He's OK,' they're thinking, 'he's one of us.' Products that never interested you before – like shortbread biscuits and Ovaltine – start appearing in your shopping trolley. You can eat most of your meals with a spoon. At parties you're not looking to chat up the talent any more; you just hope you won't get stuck in a low chair. You catch yourself humming songs from *South Pacific*. You get sudden and unaccountable urges to take up golf and eat at Harvester Restaurants. Your memory starts to let you down. You vaguely remember that one of the lasses in Abba had a nice bum, but can't recall which one. And was it the Andrews Sisters in any case? Right, where was I? Oh yes...

The Wharfe boiled and bubbled at Linton Falls, where the water has carved intriguing shapes in the limestone; it looks like sculpted meringue. In summer the water dribbles half-heartedly over the ledge, as if someone has left a tap on. But now, after rain, the water roared. A weir was built upstream of the waterfall, to ensure there was always a good head of water to turn the water-wheel of Linton Mill. At one time or another the mill processed corn, cotton, silk, flax, soap and timber. As with Low Mill at Addingham, Linton Mill has been transformed into up-market housing. Nearby is Little Emily's Bridge, a delightful and diminutive packhorse bridge, used by generations of millhands and churchgoers.

The geology of the Yorkshire Dales is a fascinating subject, no doubt, for those who like that sort of thing. But it's not for me. I have as great an interest in what goes on under my feet as I have in knowing what goes on beneath the bonnet of my car. If cleaning out the ashtray fails to make my car start, I call the AA. Some things are better left as mysteries. As far as I'm concerned, the Craven Fault could have been one of Sir William's family flaws, on a par with the Hapsburg lip and the Simpson overbite. But it's not. It's a geological shift, where the predominant rock type changes. There are a few places in the Dales – Giggleswick Scar is one, Malham Cove is another – where this fault has created dramatic landscapes. And the Craven Fault was responsible for the drop of 30 feet in the river bed at Linton Falls. You can see the change in the rock formation: shale to the south, and great scar limestone to the north.

I enjoyed a view of the falls from the modern footbridge, before taking a narrow walled path uphill – known as the Snake – to emerge at the National Park Centre, on the outskirts of Grassington. This is the National Park's HQ, where the important decisions are hammered out.

The Yorkshire Dales National Park will be fifty years old in 2004. But let's be straight about the matter: it isn't a National Park in the sense that, say, Yosemite and Yellowstone are. To start with, the Yorkshire Dales aren't owned by a grateful nation. Granted, some buildings and landscapes fall under the aegis of the National Trust. But apart from that, the National Park belongs to landowners large and small, just like anywhere else. This means that the National Park Authority is on a perpetual collision course with those who live, work and see their future in the Dales: that's some farmers and all developers.

We can thank the National Park Authority that 680 square miles of glorious landscape are unencumbered by motorways and industrial estates. Two cheers, then, for the National Park. On the other hand, there are plenty of farmers who see the National Park Authority as the enemy, dedicated to thwarting their agricultural ambitions at every turn. There are planning restrictions which, to those who farm the hills, must appear arbitrary and restrictive. It's not hard to fall foul of planning regulations; you only need to fit the wrong kind of window in a house extension or try to build a barn conveniently close to your farm instead of renovating one of the more picturesque (but redundant) field barns. It's possible to upset the National Park Authority in so many different ways. And yet, of course, it's perfectly OK to dig huge holes in the ground (and I mean *huge*), quarry for limestone and then transport it in convoys of lorries that clog up the narrow Dales roads.

In the ongoing stand-off between farmers and the National Park Authority, I take the typical *Guardian* reader's view. I weigh up all the options before coming down firmly on the fence. I am eternally grateful that our National Parks have been saved for future generations to enjoy, while having great sympathy for the farmers who feel stymied by bureaucracy and red-tape.

Sharing the car park with the National Park's offices is a Tourist Information Centre, where patient and long-suffering staff answer daft questions from the visitors, like 'What time does the park close?'

If you drop into the centre and scan some of the brochures on display, you will learn that Grassington is the 'Capital of Upper Wharfedale'. It's got shops, you see, plus an annual arts festival and little alley-ways, called 'folds', which are fun to explore. The cobbled square would be a real amenity and focal point if it wasn't always crammed with parked cars (while other cars circle the square in the vain hope that a space will somehow materialise). Despite there being a massive car park just around the corner, most folk seem unwilling or unable to walk further than from their car to the kerb. Curses on them all.

There is a fascinating little folk museum in the square, where people wander round and say things like 'Your Aunt Maude used to have one just like that, but she threw it away.' The shops are full of the stuff that people seem obliged to buy when they spend some time 'up the Dales'. It's hard to envisage a day out without coming back with a wonky hand-thrown pot or a jar of expensively over-packaged conserve, called something like Old Mother Shipton's Home-made Quince Marmalade – emanating not from a farm kitchen, of course, but from some faceless industrial estate near Middlesbrough. Grassington has all this, and more. It's even got a Spar.

Of the reasons why Grassington grew, prospered and then went into decline, little evidence remains. A lot of people visit Grassington – and other, equally picturesque Dales villages – and blithely assume that the local economy has always relied on farming. The truth is rather different, though you would have to leave the gift shops of Grassington behind in order to find it. You would need to walk up to the little road junction at the top of the village, and take Moor Road ahead. Make it a walk, not a drive, if you want to follow in the footsteps of the men, women – and, yes, children – who worked in and around the lead mines on lonely Grassington Moor.

Lead was mined throughout the Pennine hills, from the North Pennines down to the Peak District. There are huge mining fields in the steep-sided valleys of Swaledale and Arkengarthdale to the north, plus a few other sites in the Dales, of which Grassington Moor is the most extensive. Pigs of lead dating from Roman times have been unearthed, and the monks of Fountains Abbey worked a lead smelting mill here. But it wasn't until the end of the eighteenth century that the lead ore of Grassington Moor was exploited in a fully commercial way.

You can see the ruins of a smelt mill, and its underground flues – some half a mile long – which culminate at a lone chimney on a hillcrest. You can see reservoirs, dams and the many miles of watercourses created to keep a total of eight waterwheels turning. Ironically, this water was needed to power the pumps that drained water out of the mine-shafts. In the mining fields of Swaledale, shafts known as adits were driven horizontally into the hillsides. But here, on the flatter expanses of Grassington Moor, the shafts were dug straight down. The entrances are covered with metal grills now, for safety, but just gazing down into the Stygian gloom is enough to make you shudder. Whatever it is you have to do to pay the bills, just imagine climbing down there each day to scratch a living.

This was mining in its most primitive form. By the time more laboursaving devices had been invented – hydraulic rock-drills, for example – the industry was dying. For the miners of Grassington Moor, creating a labyrinth of interconnecting tunnels, it was picks and shovels all the way.

You can wander the emptiness of Grassington Moor, and imagine what it was like 150 years ago, when the industry was at its height. The most profitable year was 1865, when 2000 tons of lead were smelted. Then, in just a dozen years, the market for locally mined lead collapsed – not because demand for lead had fallen, but because it became cheaper to import it from countries such as Italy and Spain. In 1882 the last load of lead ore – known as galena – was smelted at Cupola Mill on Grassington Moor. Your powers of imagination will need to be well-honed, though, because these fascinating relics of our industrial past are quietly going back to nature.

When lead mining declined, many Dales communities – including Grassington – declined with it. Miners and their families had difficult choices to make. Some left for the coal mines of the North East.

Some stayed in the Dales and turned their hand to hill farming. Some went to work mines in the United States and elsewhere. According to census figures, the population of Grassington nose-dived from 1138 in 1851 to just 408 by the end of the century. This level of depopulation was repeated in many other parts of the Dales. Even with the proliferation of second homes and holiday cottages in recent years, the population of many communities has never recovered.

I had lunch in Grassington. It was so warm, even in October, that I sat at a table outside the pub. It was good to take my rucksack off for a breather; I asked a guy sitting at the next table if he would watch it for me. This apparently simple request takes a lot for granted, if you think about it. It means there is one person in the world who now knows that your rucksack contains something worth stealing. Worse, he knows that you will be away long enough for someone – maybe him? – to have it away. You have, in essence, given a total stranger both the opportunity and incentive to rob you. Except that, for no apparent reason, you have assumed he is a trustworthy character and not a thief at all. This displays either stunning naivety, or a touching faith in humanity. Your choice.

I'd like to think that it's our normal habit to trust people... until their behaviour makes us think otherwise. Then again, there was a time when I thought that High Street banks treated their customers with courtesy and fair-mindedness. So what the hell do I know?

'What would you like, young man?' said the landlord, when I sidled up to the bar. 'Well, I'd like you to call me 'young man' again, and then I'll have a pint.' My rucksack was there when I got back. Of course it was. I tried my brand new mobile phone again – still no joy. It didn't seem fair that I was unable to use it, when the people sitting around me were having so much fun with theirs ('What do you reckon... chips or jackets?'). Why bother engaging your companions in conversation when you could be barking inanities into a mobile phone instead?

The mountain rescue service must be thrilled at the ubiquity of mobile phones. For many years these guys have been doing sterling work, bringing injured walkers and climbers down from the fells. In theory, at least, it makes sense for walkers to carry a mobile. If they get into difficulties they can muster a hardy troupe of Chris Bonington look-alikes to bring them aid and comfort. So much for theory. In practice not every walker understands the difference between a minor inconvenience and a genuine emergency. ('You don't seem to understand, you buffoon. Our pay & display car park ticket expires in twenty minutes. *Twenty* minutes!'). Idle walkers are apt to treat the rescue volunteers as an extension of room service; some of them even have the number on their phone's speed-dialler. ('Can you airlift us a pint of milk, please? We forgot to buy any…'). And thank God for the redial button ('…Oh, and some sugar. We forgot that too.')

There was one more thing I needed to do in Grassington, which, in the context of the Dales Way, at least, is a major shopping centre. Not wanting a repeat of the previous night's nocturnal wanderings, I needed to buy a torch. I wandered into one of those shops that are stuffed from floor to ceiling with tempting outdoor stuff. It occupied a converted barn where, in 1766, John Wesley once came to preach. Of how many other outdoor shops can you say that?

There was a time when walking was a rather simpler activity than it is today. You would slip on something shapeless and warm, and just put one foot in front of the other. But those days are gone; now we scorn such a miserly approach. It seems we're more than happy to part with folding money to ensure that we look the part. Yes, folks, it's 'fashion on the fells' for the walkers of today. 'All the gear and no idea,' as the ladies in the Tourist Information Centre say, rather sniffily.

We hear the siren voices of the outdoor gear manufacturers. We're all susceptible to the adverts – especially those of us who insist we aren't. We used to buy a pair of boots or a rucksack; now we buy 'a system'. We used to buy scratchy woollen walking socks by the kilo;

now the socks are so comfortable it's like walking barefoot on shag-pile carpet.   We used to pull on a mud-coloured windjammer, made from the same low-tech, rain-attracting material from which they make bath sponges.   Now we have smart, figure-hugging garments – in this year's tastefully co-ordinated colours, naturally – which keep us striding through torrential rain long after the enjoyment has gone... just to see if a £250 cagoule really is as waterproof as the manufacturers suggest.

For that money you get a garment that not merely keeps out wind and weather, but 'breathes' too.   Hmmm, £250 is the sort of sum I spend on a car, not clothing.   And for that sort of money I'd want a jacket that could do more than breathe; I'd want it to juggle and do card tricks too.   But that's just me.

We used to find a forked stick and whittle it with a penknife.   It was something to do while waiting for the kettle to boil in the kitchen of some blighted youth hostel.   The result – after only a few hours of graft, and a couple of bandaged fingers – was a home-made walking-stick.   Marvellous.   Now we go to an outdoor shop instead and pick up a telescopic pole in lightweight titanium, with three sections, an ergonomic handle with a built-in compass and – a sign of the times – an instruction manual.

We spurn something as simple as a penknife, in favour of a Swiss Army Knife.   Isn't it somehow typical of the Swiss that their army should be famous not for a successful military campaign, but for precision-made cutlery?   You can still buy a Swiss Army Knife with just a couple of blades, but only a skinflint would be content with that.   The knives recline seductively in display cases at your local out-door shop.   Like the brazen denizens of some red-light district, the pleasures become more exotic with every fiver you're prepared to fork out.   Corkscrew, saw, screwdriver, magnifying glass and that pointy thing that nobody knows what to do with.   Towards the top of the range – it's serious 'three-in-a-waterbed' money now – you get a watch, hedge trimmer, arc welder and full internet connection... plus a smart leather case on wheels to keep it in.   You want one.   You know you do.   But if you have to ask the price, you really can't afford one.

Now that everyone – even me – has a mobile phone, some outdoorsy folk with more money than sense are splashing out on GPS devices (that's 'global positioning system', if you please). They no longer have to make do with vague generalisations about where they are: up shit creek without a paddle, say, or between a rock and a hard place. The trouble is that they are relying on these gizmos instead of resorting to tried and tested methods: being fit, well clad and shod, and being able to read a map. With a GPS, they know where they are to three decimal places. It's just a shame they probably haven't the slightest idea what these numbers actually mean.

What about a digital altimeter? In the good old days a doomed mountaineer would consign his thoughts to paper: 'Here I am, halfway up a mountain, and gangrene is setting in...' Now, armed with an altimeter, a mountaineer can be pedantically accurate, as he composes that last letter to his loved ones: 'Here I am, at exactly 6176 metres above sea level, and gangrene is setting in...' Think what a comfort that would be.

Yes, you find things in these outdoor shops that you didn't even know you needed. How about a tiny, basic, army-issue tin-opener that, after just a few minutes hard work, will remove the lid, leaving a rim so sharp and jagged that it could slice a finger straight off? Or 'Jungle-strength' insect repellent? Why, when the most venomous insect you're likely to encounter is a drowsy wasp? How about an ergonomic rucksack that comes with a company mission statement? Or waterproof matches: a needless extravagance when there's a bloke in every town centre who will sell you ten lighters for a quid.

It's a guy thing. We're not just going for a walk; in our minds we're mountain men from Montana, armed and paranoid, ready to survive a nuclear winter or take on the Government in a shooting war. These are toys for the boys: the kind of men whose one great regret is that they've never lived through a war. What I mean is a proper war: one of the old-fashioned kind where the enemy fights back.

I can lust after overpriced gadgets as much as the next man, but all I needed on this occasion was the torch. Of the type I wanted, though, there was only one left. It was water-resistant to a depth of 50 feet, and I was expecting rain. So that was good. But it was in an unpleasant khaki camouflage colour, and that was bad. If I dropped it on the grass, I'd probably never find it again. Oh well...

The riverside path runs out of steam soon after leaving Grassington. So Dales Way walkers have to take a high-level route instead. I walked up to the little crossroads at the top of the village, turning left by the town hall onto Chapel Lane. My imagination kicked in where the lane petered out. It was here, in 1766, that Tom Lee murdered the village doctor, Richard Petty, and threw his body into the Wharfe. Tom Lee was a bit of a bad lot, by all accounts: a blacksmith by trade, but a thief and a poacher by inclination. The doctor let Tom know that he was under suspicion. After an altercation in a local pub, Tom Lee and his apprentice lay in wait for the doctor, who was making his way back home in the dark. It was Tom Lee who dealt the doctor the fatal blow, but it took both men to dispose of the corpse.

Twice Lee was tried for the murder; twice he was found not guilty. At the third trial the blacksmith's apprentice could live with his conscience no longer, and turned King's evidence. Lee was hanged at York and then – this is the chilling bit – his body was hung in chains at the site of the murder. Tom Lee's bleached bones remained here for four years as a fateful warning to others intent on bad business.

A high-level stroll was fine by me, and for the rest of the day I traversed one of the finest limestone landscapes in the Dales. What a treat. Immediately out of Grassington – and marked on the map as Lea Green – are the remains of a Romano-British settlement. It sounds exciting, but, to a layman such as me, with archaeological expertise limited to watching Tony Robinson of 'Time Team' trying to escape from the shadow of Baldrick and his 'cunning plans', I'm afraid it's just a few lumps and bumps in the grass.

I skirted the top of Grass Wood: a rare example of an ash wood on limestone. In summer it's a wonderful oasis of wild flowers and birdsong. This is my kind of walking country: knuckles of rock pushing through the springy, sheep-cropped grass; drystone walls snaking sinuously across the fells; limestone scars studded with stunted but tenacious little trees.

I approached a broad, breezy expanse of limestone pavement above the superb dry valley of Conistone Dib. This is one of my favourite places in the Dales: an almost lunar landscape of clints (they're the limestone blocks) and grikes (they're the fissures in between the clints), which enjoys panoramic views across the broad valley of the Wharfe. And at those times when better-known limestone pavements – on top of Malham Cove, for example – are overcrowded, this is one place where you can find a bit of peace and quiet.

More than half of the country's limestone pavements are to be found here in the Yorkshire Dales National Park. That's something to celebrate. But we have been chipping away at them for years, just so that gardeners can surround their herbaceous borders with artistically weathered rockeries. And that desecration should make us hang our heads in shame. I don't understand this gardening fetish: the idea that rocks look better in suburbia than where they've been lying for, oh, the last few million years. But then I don't understand why people pick wild flowers either, just to watch them wither in a vase. And then there is flower arranging: what a strange notion. Flowers don't *need* arranging, for God's sake. They look fine the way they are. Alive, preferably. And if they're adding a swathe of colour to some Dales flower meadow, so much the better.

Thankfully, and not before time, we now seem to appreciate just how rare these limestone pavements are, and how easily they can be destroyed. Preservation orders have been slapped on many of these distinctive landscape features. If I had to choose between conserving a limestone pavement, or a stately home built by some pampered aristocrat who made his money from grinding the faces of the poor into the dirt... well, there's just no contest, is there?

These limestone pavements certainly appeal to photographers, which is why I was contacted, out of the blue, by an advertising agency in Florida. When I'm not writing books, I'm a landscape photographer by trade, and among the pictures displayed on my website were shots of pavements. The guy (I'll call him Greg, because that was his name) explained that his company was producing a television advert. It was to be one of those hi-tech extravaganzas, utilising just about every visual trick in the book. Dolphins would leap up waterfalls and turn into butterflies, and a beautiful woman would walk across an expanse of limestone pavement and… well, I rather lost track after that. But you get the general idea.

The upshot was that Greg wanted to fly to Yorkshire for three days, to get pictures of limestone pavements. What he wanted were sequences of still shots that, by means of computer wizardry, could later be dovetailed into the animated advert. I was to act as both photographer and guide. I named my price, Greg agreed, and a few days later we met up for breakfast at his hotel in Skipton. Having exchanged so many emails in a brief but breathless correspondence, we greeted each other like long-lost friends.

So far so good. As we tucked into our full English breakfasts, we pored over maps and discussed picture ideas. Greg described what he wanted, and I earmarked a handful of likely locations. Outside the window the sun disappeared behind a long bank of grey cloud. We laughed about the inclement English weather ('Spring?' I said, 'It's more like winter!') and set off in his hired car on a startlingly cold April morning. But even with frost still on the ground, I couldn't foresee any major problems.

First we photographed the limestone pavement at Malham Cove. Since there were to be no people in the shots, I was glad the chilly weather had kept visitors away. We investigated some other pavements around the Three Peaks before having lunch at the Station Inn at Ribblehead. Through the pub window the weather was looking decidedly wintry: hail, sleet, flurries of snow, from a sky the colour of unpolished pewter. I apologised for the weather, like it was my fault.

The ever-affable Greg just laughed. It was going to take more than bad weather to dampen his enthusiasm for the job in hand. We finished off our giant Yorkshire puddings ('The English pizza', I explained to him), and headed off towards Wharfedale. We walked uphill from the tiny village of Conistone, as the snow whipped around our heads. Had I been on my own, I would have turned back there and then. But on this occasion I was just the Sherpa; Greg was holding the purse-strings, and he seemed keen to carry on regardless.

By the time we reached the limestone pavement, we were caught in a blizzard. I thought I was in one of those *Reader's Digest* articles: 'I Faced the Frozen Hell and Lived.' Greg and I were dressed for typical spring weather in the Dales. We were prepared for sunshine or showers... but not for snow. Greg ploughed on, looking for suitable camera angles. As he viewed the disappearing landscape through the little rectangle made by his thumbs and forefingers, I began to question his sanity. Then, just for the sake of balance, I began to question my own. The jury was out on both counts.

Once the visibility was down to a few feet, even Greg began to realise what I'd known for some time: that we were in a bit of bother. The snow had created a total white-out; with no visible landmarks we were utterly disorientated. We might have been only a mile or so, as the crow flies, from warmth, safety and a pint of Theakston's Bitter at the Tennants Arms in Kilnsey. But at that moment it might as well have been 100 miles. The landscape of Wharfedale – so pastoral, so familiar – suddenly seemed very threatening.

Even the irrepressible Greg had stopped smiling by now. Buffeted by driving snow, we sought shelter behind some rocks. A limestone pavement is no place to be when you can't see where you're going. One false step into a grike, and you've got a broken ankle to add to your troubles. Greg was starting to shiver. No one knew where we were. I convinced myself we were going to die, though I tried to keep my mounting despair to myself. 'Got any ID on you?' I asked Greg, trying to find an unconcerned tone of voice. 'Yeah. Why?' 'Oh, no particular reason...' My voice trailed off into the teeth of the wind.

With nothing to see but snow, strange thoughts and questions crept unbidden into my mind. Scientists insist that no two snow crystals are alike. But how do they know? Have Wagon Wheels got smaller over the years, or is it just that we've got bigger? Why don't we have a 99p coin? Think how useful it would be. Why don't film censors get depraved and corrupt? Why is there a 'best by' date on sour cream? Why on earth do we have to wait '28 days for delivery'? Most baffling of all, whatever happened to the Bermuda Triangle? Back in the 1970s ships and planes were vanishing on a daily basis. And now it's disappeared. Just like that. Weird...

Well, if our lifeless bodies were going to be found – huddled pathetically together – when the snow eventually thawed, I wanted to have at least one half-decent picture in my camera. 'I'm just going to take a snap,' I said to Greg, who was huddled in a foetal position. 'I may be some time.'

Into that monochromatic moonscape I staggered, camera bag suspended from my neck like an albatross. After a few minutes I found an intriguingly spare composition of limestone pavement, a rock and a solitary tree. The wind was buffeting so strongly that I had to put all my weight against the tripod to stop it from being blown over. I rattled off a few frames with a grim kind of satisfaction, before retracing my steps to exchange doomed pleasantries with the sheltering Greg. His weak smile revealed a set of chattering teeth.

It was almost time to scribble the last notes to our loved ones: heartfelt things we wished we had expressed years before. But then, as quickly as it had started, the blizzard abated. The snow stopped, the clouds parted and a shaft of spring sunshine illuminated the flanks of Wharfedale and made the snow sparkle like diamonds.

Yes, we'd faced that frozen hell, and lived to tell the tale. Once we'd traipsed back down into Conistone, found the car, and headed back towards Skipton with the heater on full blast, we realised what a close shave it had been. Dressed for April showers, we'd been totally unprepared for blizzard conditions. It was foolish – we knew it now – and we'd been lucky.

The pictures Greg eventually used were, ironically, the very first set, from the top of Malham Cove. As for 'my' picture: well, it looks so peaceful, so still, so other-worldly, with not a hint of the storm that was raging at the time. And they say the camera never lies...

It was good to see the limestone pavement again – but this time on a bright autumn day, with no immediate danger of being buried by a snowdrift. I passed Conistone Pie: a prominent limestone outcrop that's totally natural and not, as it first appears, a hilltop fortress. Down below, in the valley, I could see Kilnsey Crag, one of Wharfedale's best-loved landmarks. At 170 feet high, and with a wicked overhang, the crag has long been a challenge for climbers. The overhang was first negotiated in 1957, using all the equipment at a climber's disposal. Until 1989 no one had ever thought to climb it freestyle: no one sane, anyway. That was the year that Mark Leach, a young climber from Lancashire, waltzed up in a matter of minutes: a stunning achievement. The very thought of it makes my hands clammy, even now, as I tap away, one-fingered, at my computer, like a demented woodpecker.

I'm no climber. Even looking at pictures of climbers can bring on feelings of vertigo. You may think I'm joking, but I'm not. The whole concept of free-climbing is so alien to me that my brain cannot compute images of incredibly fit young lads – and lasses – clinging to a rockface – with nothing more than a handhold the size of a marrowfat pea between them and a premature appointment with the grim reaper.

My dad used to tell a story about the time he and some friends suspended a grand piano from the top of Kilnsey Crag. I never thought to ask him that vital question – 'Why?' – and it's too late to ask him now.

Close to the crag is Kilnsey Park, the main attraction of which is a fishing lake. It is stocked with trout in surreal quantities. If you toss a handful of breadcrumbs in, the water boils with fish: millions of them. Fishermen stand around the lake, casting their lines. I use the word 'fishermen' loosely; it would be hard for anyone to bait a hook and not catch a fish. The recreational value seems minimal: just one step away from shooting fish in the proverbial barrel. When I was a kid I used to have a fishing game. We dangled toy rods baited with magnets into a cardboard 'pond' full of cardboard fish with staples in their heads. By no reckoning was it a game of skill; every time we waggled the rod, we 'caught' a fish. The fishermen at Kilnsey fishery obviously like the same kind of odds, the poor saps.

The Kilnsey of today may only be a compact cluster of houses, but it hosts the largest agricultural show in Wharfedale. It's held on the level pasture (once a post-glacial lake) between Kilnsey and Conistone, on the Tuesday after August Bank Holiday. There's a punishing fell-race to the top of Kilnsey Crag and back, for people with more energy than sense. A wall gets knocked down and rebuilt every year during a competition that tests the skills of the local drystone wallers. They labour away, almost in the shadow of the crag, while the crowds watch the sheep dog trials and admire the displays of fruit, vegetables and home-made produce. The competition categories remain reassuringly traditional: so it's 'three English apples', 'six broad beans' and 'pot of home-made lemon curd'... rather than 'three mobile phones' or 'six website portals'.

The show attracts an eclectic mixture of people. Farmers get a chance to socialise and sink a few pints in the beer tent. Visitors stand out, in their colourful cagoules, from the local landowners, who feel no such need to court fashion. These local worthies shop at stalls offering 'Mud-coloured Clothing for the Gentry'; their understated uniform seems to say 'I don't *walk* in the countryside... I own it.'

There are stalls devoted to the contentious delights of rural pursuits: 'field sports' to those who follow the hounds, 'blood sports' to those who take a more sanguine view. You can buy picturesque placemats – showing saboteurs being soundly thrashed by men in hunting pink – and add your signature to a petition:

We, the undersigned, wish to maintain our traditional right to hunt foxes. If these animals weren't hunted, the delicate ecological balance would be upset. We are conservationists. We love foxes. And the way we express our love for these fascinating animals is by hunting them down, killing them and daubing their blood on our children's faces.

Hunting and hypocrisy go hand in hand. What particularly grates – with me, anyway – is the dishonesty of the hunting lobby. On the one hand they insist that hunting with hounds is the most efficient and humane way to cull foxes. On the other hand they try to mollify the animal lovers by suggesting that most foxes get away. Well, they can't have it both ways. If what they say is true, then they aren't merely bloodthirsty... they're bloodthirsty and inefficient. I'd have more respect for the hunters if they just came clean and admitted that they enjoy the chase, and get a quasi-sexual thrill out of watching a fox being torn limb from limb by a pack of hounds. And let's not forget the horse thing too...

We were promised an outright ban on hunting with dogs. Unfortunately, the Government has suddenly realised that even a buffoon in a pink jacket is able to scrawl a cross on a ballot paper. Yes, the noise you can hear is New Labour casting their manifesto pledges to the four winds. Prepare yourself for one unsatisfactory compromise or another.

Maybe the 'sport' could be downgraded to fox *hurting*: such a slight change of emphasis and spelling that most people wouldn't even notice. Foxes could be beaten up, warned about their future conduct and released back into the community. Or we could follow the sterling example of the Quorn Hunt, by chasing a pale, tasteless meat substitute over hill and dale. Or – and this is my preferred option – we could stop hunting foxes and start hunting minor members of the Royal Family instead. Imagine: two social problems solved, at a stroke. The dogs would get a run out, the Civil List would be brought down to a manageable size and the Government could get back to what they do best: being beastly to foreigners and driving another nail into the coffin of the NHS. A good result all round.

Right, I'll get down off my high horse now. Stay up there too long and you run the risk of altitude sickness.

Branching away from the main valley is Littondale, which is every bit as beautiful as Wharfedale. From my path, hugging the edge of a limestone scar, I had a panoramic view of the valley, with its river – no, not the Litton, but the Skirfare – pootling down to join the Wharfe at Amerdale Dub, which sounds like a hardcore remix of some interminable dance track. The side-dale is named after Litton, one of the villages in the valley. The neighbouring village of Arncliffe was one of the locations used for 'Emmerdale Farm', when it was an unassuming soap about farming, and before it started competing with the other soaps to see just how much rape, violence, murder, incest, adultery, blackmail, and hot girl-on-girl lesbian action could be crammed into a drama that was ostensibly about a diminutive Dales community.

Where the River Skirfare meets the Wharfe, there's a sign in a field: 'Car parking £1.' And, despite the fact that there is nothing here of great note, and no particular reason why visitors should park here (and pay) rather than park elsewhere (for free), there is often a handful of parked cars to be seen. Perhaps people are reassured by having to pay, as they have to do in towns and cities. It gives them a warm, comfortable, familiar feeling, as they're unscrewing the top from the Thermos flask and sharing out the Sunday supplements.

It was a delight to walk along the limestone scars, before dropping down into Kettlewell. In late afternoon sunshine, with smoke billowing from almost every chimney, it was a welcoming sight: the archetypal Dales village.

Kettlewell Youth Hostel confirmed my booking, thank goodness. I'm a big fan of youth hostels. They've played their part, over the years, in introducing townies to the joys of walking in the country. 'Walking', please note, not 'living'. As I parked my rucksack in a small, single-sex dormitory, I savoured the pungent odours of damp socks, cheap deodorant and athlete's foot powder, mingling with the sour vestiges of unrestrained flatulence. There's an appealing atmosphere of asceticism and self-denial about hostels, along with the chance to meet people who take their walking very seriously indeed. And, down in the kitchen, you can watch a guy with a small tin of kidney beans trying to beg, borrow or steal the other ingredients he needs to make a bowl of chilli con carne.

Youth hostels are trying to change with the times. It's goodbye and good riddance to the bad old days of curfews, rubber sheets and escape committees. These days you can even book family rooms. And there's no need to hide the car any more – like some guilty secret – and pretend that you arrived on foot. But I wouldn't want hostels to become *too* comfortable; it's good to wear that hair shirt once in a while. I have fond memories of taking my own kids youth hostelling in the Dales. In addition to the basic charge, hostellers were expected to help with the chores. On the morning after one rather boisterous evening, I asked the guy in charge what jobs we could do. 'Just take those kids away,' he said, wearily, 'and we'll call it quits.'

There are still three inns in Kettlewell; two of them, the Racehorses and the Blue Bell, face up to each other by the bridge over Park Gill Beck. I checked them all out. Stone-flagged floors: check. Open fires: check. Horse-brasses: check. Exposed beams: check. Cheerful ambience: check. Tempting menu: check. I had a steaming plateful of 'beef casserole, cooked in Black Sheep Bitter': a good beer to make a casserole with. By the time I'd wiped the last of the gravy off my chin, and gazed mindlessly into the fire, I was ready for bed.

Back at the hostel, I lay in my bunk, enjoying an impromptu display of synchronised farting, and the 'call and response' of two heavy snorers, before drifting off into a dreamless sleep.

Day Four

KETTLEWELL TO RIBBLEHEAD

Yockenthwaite

K ettlewell is a typical Dales village, in that it was built up around crossroads and a river bridge. Lying on the old coaching road from Richmond to London, the village once boasted five inns, a beerhouse and a weekly market. Coaches heading for Richmond had to tackle the perilous gradient of Park Rash, a road which heads off into Wensleydale by way of wild and windswept Coverdale. This road is perhaps the nearest the Yorkshire Dales get to a mountain pass; at its steepest it's an unforgiving 1 in 4. If it was hard getting horse-drawn carriages *up* this road, God knows how they managed to get them *down* in one piece. The brakes must have been smoking. Lathered horses may not labour up Park Rash any more, but you can tell that Kettlewell is another much-visited Dales village by the size of its car park. The road barely touches the village; you need to explore on foot, as I did, briefly, on that Monday morning.

Kettlewell is undeniably pretty. And that name is a bonus: better than Grimethorpe, eh? The old stone cottages are full of character; they blend into their surroundings with a harmony that you find in few other places. These houses just look *right*. Yes, when jaded townies visit the Yorkshire Dales, Kettlewell is the sort of place they fall in love with. But, as with so many other liaisons, this love affair is likely to be based on fantasy. Drunken glances across a crowded room; a furtive grope out on the dance floor; some coquettish flirtation by candlelight; words whispered out of longing and loneliness. Then, before they know what's hit them, townies are smitten. They start checking out the estate agents' windows and planning a new life in the Dales.

Country life holds great attractions for city folk who, almost by definition, know nothing at all about it. What they fall for is a rose-tinted vision of Arcadia, the soft-focus romanticism of a shampoo advert. Weary of selling their souls to some multinational corporation, commuting from the blandness of suburbia, they're looking to get back to nature. The country life – spent dead-heading roses, trimming hedges and quaffing schooners of cream sherry – looks an attractive option to jaded wage slaves. They long for the trappings of the countryside: a picturesque cottage, an Aga, green wellies, a brace of black labradors, a Range Rover with mud streaks that aren't stuck on, and one of those 'farmhouse kitchens' they've seen in some glossy lifestyle magazine.

But appearances can be deceptive. Townies looking to swap the crime and grime of the city for what they fondly imagine will be a rural idyll, are setting themselves up for disappointment. Men who have earned their money in town tend to see the countryside as a recreational amenity: an extension of the gym and the wine bar, where stressed-out executives can unwind by drinking in a gorgeous view (preferably through the windscreen of a stationary Range Rover) and reciting a restorative mantra of FT indices. Their wives imagine themselves traipsing around the herb garden in a Laura Ashley frock, with a basket of meadow flowers hung decorously over one arm.

Men dream of a less-acquisitive lifestyle in the country, unaware that the competitive flame can't be doused so easily. Having spent their formative years stuck in rush-hour traffic, extending the hand (or, at least, the middle digit) of friendship to their fellow drivers, they find that driving in the country is not as much fun as the car manufacturers would have them believe. It's frustrating to crawl for mile after twisty mile in the slippery wake of a slurry-laden tractor, whose driver regards traffic signals of any kind as entirely optional.

The love affair seldom lasts. The novelty of living in the country generally wears off after about six weeks... and the pleasure fades soon after. Aspects of country life that initially seemed quaint and endearing soon begin to irritate. For one thing it's so bloody noisy. Farmers don't talk to each other; they shout. Their dogs bark all night. The apprentice bell-ringers in the village church spend every Sunday morning trying, in vain, to orchestrate some rudimentary peal. Even the monotonous bleating of grazing sheep can bring on a migraine.

Townies are appalled that the countryside smells of shit rather than fabric softener. And it's a mess, frankly. There's farm machinery quietly rusting away in the corners of every field. And is it really necessary to have so many dead animals lying around the place?

They come to realise that a genuine farmhouse kitchen looks more like an abattoir or a car-breaker's yard. And if they so much as mention the noise or the smell or the mud, they're likely to find that the waggonload of sinus-clearing slurry has been tipped outside their front door.

When townies come to live in the Dales, they look forward to having a few picturesque yokels around the place, to add a sense of scale and a little local colour. But the ruddy-faced farmers are surly and monosyllabic. They don't even doff their caps, or, if they do, it's merely to wave them in a sarcastic parody of deference. Instead of doing unspeakable things to semi-domesticated animals, shouldn't farmers be leaning on gates, chewing straw and misdirecting lost motorists? For townies accustomed to being surrounded at work by toadies, lackeys and lickspittles, it's disheartening to come home to nothing but scorn, slurry and sedition.

Trying to ingratiate themselves with the locals, many newcomers take up country pursuits. Men develop an unhealthy interest in killing small defenceless animals – dispatching them with a Purdey shotgun, pack of hounds or a light, last-minute touch on the power steering. Women attend WI meetings: draughty evenings in village halls entering Most Exciting Tea Towel Competitions.

It doesn't work. After a few months of attempted integration, the newcomers find themselves spending more and more of their leisure hours with other disheartened exiles from the city. Over the course of liquor-fuelled evenings they can let down their defences and admit that the much-vaunted attractions of country life are just lies and innuendo, shamelessly propagated by estate agents and the editors of those glossy lifestyle magazines. Amongst friends they'll mutter conspiratorially about terse, unfriendly farmers who seem to appear – at any moment, without warning, their clothes in disarray – from sheepfold and byre.

Talk usually turns to the attractions of the city: the very same lifestyle the townies were so keen to abandon just a few months earlier. Shallow, meaningless relationships with other overpaid financiers never looked as good as they do now. Yes, once the newcomers have taken off those rose-tinted spectacles, it can be the devil of a job to find them again.

For the locals, the appearance of a removal van is worth a muted cheer. It means that another defeated family is packing up their goods, chattels and dreams of country living, and heading back to wherever they came from. Another 'For Sale' sign will appear on the cottage, with a price tag that locals can no longer afford. Another family of townies will be seduced by the prospect of life in the Dales. Perhaps they'll have no sense of smell. Perhaps they'll be as deaf as the posts that line the village greens. For their sake, let's hope so.

Village life in the Yorkshire Dales is nothing like 'The Archers'. In summer it's far too busy. Day-trippers drive all the way up to places like Kettlewell, just to check what their new in-car stereo system sounds like. As anyone living within 5 miles can testify, it sounds like a man armed with a leg of lamb trying to break out of an IKEA wardrobe. In contrast, winters are quiet. Dead quiet. Nothing happens... and it happens so slowly.

Think twice about moving to your dream cottage with roses round the door. Then think again. Then dismiss the idea altogether. Enjoy a day in the Dales – maybe a long weekend – and then do yourself a favour and bugger off home.

The best view of Kettlewell is probably from Old Cote Pasture, the flank of hill that divides Wharfedale from neighbouring Littondale. From this high vantage the village fits snugly into its surroundings, astride its own beck and dwarfed by fells. The village grew up around the old stone bridge, the houses huddled tightly together Beyond them are small fields, neatly delineated by drystone walls; longer, straighter walls head unerringly up the fellsides. Here, and elsewhere in Wharfedale, are many examples of medieval strip-farming systems, known as lynchets. The best time to see them is early or late in the day, when raking sunshine makes them stand out most prominently.

Kettlewell's busiest days came when lead was being mined. While a few houses bear seventeenth-century datestones, most were rebuilt during the nineteenth century. The Norman church, too, was so heavily restored during Victoria's reign that few traces of the earlier building remain. There were weekly markets here, and three fairs each year. To counteract the feeling that it used to be a rather more vibrant place than it is today, Kettlewell now has its own scarecrow festival every summer. And it's welcome to it, frankly.

Wandering around the village I saw a hand-written sign: 'Don't empty your dog here, £500 fine, CCTV cameras.' Rather fanciful, of course, but heartfelt nevertheless. Someone should apply for a research grant to investigate the stubbornly adhesive ingredient that makes dog shit so hard to shift from the tread of a pair of walking boots. Another sign, written in the same despairing hand, read:

'Don't even think about parking here.' Here was someone, I felt, who was not blessed with the sunniest of dispositions. Someone who might benefit from some gentle therapy. Or a slap.

As I left Kettlewell, under grey and gloomy skies, I felt I was leaving the lower dale behind too. The weekend walkers were gone. I knew there were many miles to cover before reaching the bunk-barn at Cam Houses, my refuge for the night. I had taken the opportunity of phoning ahead to book a bed – from a phone box, of course, not my accursed mobile. I called a number I'd been given – it was in Leeds, of all places – to be told, unambiguously, by a friendly female voice, 'Just turn up there, you'll be fine.' Thus reassured, I crossed the bridge over the Wharfe and rejoined the riverside path.

I was just getting into my stride... and then it happened. A sudden, visceral, cataclysmic roar that thundered inside my skull like a thermo-nuclear device. I thought Armageddon had come, and that my head was going to explode like an overripe watermelon. It took me a few seconds – utterly disoriented, loose-bowelled and scared witless – to realise it wasn't the end of the world as we know it, after all, but just a plane.

The RAF use the Yorkshire Dales to practise their low-flying manoeuvres, you see. Flying in and out of these narrow valleys probably didn't prepare their pilots too well for desert combat during the Gulf War. But if we were ever to declare war on, say, North Wales – never an option to dismiss out of hand – our boys will be ready. I understand that fighter pilots have to learn their craft somewhere. But a National Park? What role can sonic booms possibly play in the promotion of 'quiet recreation'?

The Dales Way path ran in a straight line here – from one field to another, across a series of ladder stiles. Walking was easy, although soggy, once I'd calmed down a bit and re-established which way was up. About the time my fillings stopped rattling, I passed the little village of Starbotton. The village keeps a respectful distance from its neighbours; a quick glance at the Ordnance Survey map confirms that Wharfedale villages are typically about 2 miles apart. Starbotton is built just above the river's floodplain; this did not save the village in 1686, though, when Cam Beck flooded disastrously.

In these upper reaches, with the head of the valley coming into view, Wharfedale presents itself as the archetypal U-shaped valley, with drystone walls, field barns and scattered trees – overlooked by limestone scars and the expanse of Buckden Pike and Birks Fell. It seems, at first sight, to be a timeless scene.

There's a belief shared by many visitors that the Yorkshire Dales are unchanged and unchanging. But they haven't always looked the way they do now. Indeed, over the last millennium, change has been the only constant. Upper Wharfedale, for example, used to be a hunting forest – a 'chase' – where noblemen would hunt the king's deer. The forest has since been cleared, leaving just a few scattered copses behind like the stubble of a careless shaver.

It's hard to imagine Wharfedale without all the field barns and drystone walls. Yet these are, in fact, some of the most recent additions to the Dales landscape. Only a halfwit would try to explain this complex sociological shift in a single paragraph... so here goes. The common land that surrounded townships and villages was gradually taken into private ownership. A succession of Enclosures Acts aimed to replace what had been essentially a peasant economy, with a more efficient use of the land. To establish their rights of ownership, farmers were obliged to meet the expense of enclosing fields. Those who couldn't afford this work would find their allotments being sold off, cheaply, to neighbouring landowners. This meant that the rich got richer, by annexing the best land, while the poor got poorer, by losing their traditional rights of pasture on what had been common land. So no change there, then. The rural poor swapped the freedom to scratch a bare living in the country for the opportunity to starve, or scratch a bare living in more urban surroundings. For a lot of people the choice was stark but clear: work as farm labourers for the landed gentry, or as millhands in the industrial towns of the North.

A wise old folk song presents similar sentiments, in a more graphic way:

The law doth punish man or woman
That steals the goose from off the common,
But lets the greater felon loose,
That steals the common from the goose.

For enclosing the fells, there wasn't a wide choice of materials. After the forest clearances, wood was hard to find. Hedges take a long time to become established and sheep-proof; on higher pastures they hardly grow at all. But there was no shortage of rocks; fields had to be cleared of stones in any case. So drystone walling it was. Walls may have been expensive to build initially, but by gum they were built to last.

The Enclosures Acts laid down strict criteria for the building of stone walls. They stipulated the height of the wall, its width at both base and top, and the number of 'through' stones per yard of wall. There were typically two layers of 'through' stones, at heights of about 2 feet and 4 feet; they extended the full width of the wall, or beyond, and helped to bind both sides together. The wall was topped with a layer of capstones, almost always without cement or mortar. If a wall 'settled', the capstones would 'settle' too. A well-built wall is a structure in equilibrium; with timely maintenance it will stand for hundreds of years. So don't be clambering over the farmers' walls; use the gates and stiles instead.

I have my own – and no doubt overly simplistic – dating system for these drystone walls. The smallest fields and enclosures – often of irregular shape – that surround farms and villages, are mostly from the sixteenth and seventeenth centuries. Whereas the neater, more uniform field walls are a result of the various Enclosures Acts of the late-eighteenth and early-ninteenth centuries. The long, straight walls that climb up the fellsides and disappear over the moor tops were some of the last to be built. The old roads, used mainly by drovers and trains of packhorses, were defined by walls on both sides – with the happy result that these traffic-free thoroughfares are still available to the walkers of today. By 1850 the work of walling the Dales was done.

Many voices were raised in protest. Ironically, most of them objected to the change of land use on aesthetic grounds. This unique landscape would be changed for ever, they wailed, if the Dales were to be parcelled up into walled fields. And now, a mere 150–200 years after most of the walls in the Dales were built, we can hardly imagine this landscape without them.

It's the same with the field barns that seem to occupy the corner of every field. Despite being fascinating examples of vernacular architecture, most of them are as superfluous to modern farming requirements as the shire-horse and the scythe. Don't get me wrong: I love the patterns of walls and barns. But, on the other hand, I don't want the Yorkshire Dales to become just another outpost of theme-park Britain.

There comes a point when we can no longer turn the clock back or perhaps a better analogy – stop the clock at any particular hour. The Dales should not be ossified in the condition we find them at the start of the twenty-first century, any more than we should disconnect farmhouses from the National Grid or put those heavy horses back into harness.

The Dales did not become the way they look today by trying to halt progress, otherwise we might now be trying to save tracts of hunting forest or unenclosed pasture. There are grants available, in some parts of the Dales, to encourage farmers to keep the barns in good repair. And why? Presumably because they look pretty. Yet these same farmers may not be able to build what they actually need: an extension to a milking parlour, say, or a silo.

My opinion (and worth about as much as you paid for it) is that new uses should be found for some of these redundant field barns. There seems little point in making them look presentable, if they serve no useful purpose. We shouldn't convert them into houses, though, apart from those barns that lie within existing village boundaries. But we can always use more camping barns, offering cheap accommodation for walkers on a tight budget. Perhaps a few barns could be converted into 'tele-cottages' and workshops. Or maybe the brothels and bawdy houses which so many Dales communities lack. So what about all the other barns? Well, I'm afraid we're going to have to let them fall down. There just aren't enough grants to save them all. Sorry.

I soon arrived in Buckden, another village built just above the Wharfe's floodplain. The last village in Wharfedale, Buckden has a charming 'back of beyond-ish' feel. Once it was the centre of the hunting forest of Langstrothdale Chase. Even the village pub is called the Buck Inn, though these days you are more likely to see peacocks than deer. At Buckden the valley divides into two. If you were to go right, you would follow the road past the White Lion at Cray, then climb steeply up to Fleet Moss – at 1934ft, the highest stretch of road in Yorkshire – before descending first into Bishopdale, then Wensleydale. The Dales Way bears left, to follow the Wharfe into lovely Langstrothdale.

Anglian settlers established most of the villages in Wharfedale, during the sixth and seventh centuries. Names such as Burnsall, Appletreewick, Grassington and Kettlewell betray their Anglian origins. Nordic settlers, coming later, during the tenth century, often had to settle further up each valley, at higher altitudes, wherever they could find land to farm. Beyond Buckden the farm-hamlets were created by Norsemen, which accounts for such mellifluous names as Yockenthwaite and Beckermonds.

Upper Wharfedale is another favourite spot of mine. A limestone scar rears up at the end of the valley; the view from the top, looking back down Wharfedale, is like sitting in the grandstand of a stadium. The walk that links Buckden, Cray and Hubberholme would be high on my list of Desert Island Walks: easy walking, classic views and a choice of good pubs at all three points of the triangle. On this occasion I had lunch at The George in Hubberholme, a pub which oozes character. I propped up my pack, eased myself into a high-backed pew and was entertained by an excitable bunch of Norfolk folk who were having more fun ordering lunch than you would imagine was possible.

There's a pleasantly symbiotic relationship between walkers and pubs. Many of these delightfully situated pubs would have gone out of business long ago if it hadn't been for the hobnail-booted brigade of happy wanderers. Isolated pubs were built to service a very different clientele: the drovers were a notoriously thirsty crew, the packhorse men too. Pubs were built on the junction of well-used tracks – it stands to reason – even if those tracks have disappeared, or are now used only by recreational walkers.

A pint or two is the traditional reward after a good walk, and the traditional consolation after a cheerless trudge through driving rain. But walkers don't pack any alcohol for the trip. Years ago, before I'd learned the finer points of the walking game, I rambled around the Dales with a mate and a bottle of whisky. The walkers we met were horrified to be offered a swig, and backed off from any contact with us. It was almost as though we'd suggested gang-banging a particularly attractive cow, like poor libidinous Frank.

There isn't much to Hubberholme, but what there is is damn near perfect. The stone bridge over the Wharfe comprises a single, graceful arch. At one time it was a river crossing on an old trading road that linked the market towns of Lancaster and Newcastle. So important was this route that when the bridge was repaired in 1659, the cost was met by the whole of the West Riding of Yorkshire.

The George stands like a sentry at one end of the bridge, with the church of St Michael and All Angels at the other. It is everything a Dales church should be – small, squat, with a square tower, and roofed with lead from local mines – in a delectable setting. The church doorway is framed by a pair of ancient yew trees. The writer JB Priestley loved Hubberholme. It is 'one of the smallest and pleasantest places in the world', he wrote. The man who created smoky Bruddersford chose this churchyard to have his ashes scattered. I can only applaud his taste.

I made time to spend a few tranquil minutes in the church. Famously, this is one of only two churches in Yorkshire – the other is in Flamborough – still to have its rood loft intact. Hubberholme's is carved with the date it was made – 1558 – by the carpenter, William Jake (we know his name because he carved that too, as any proud craftsman should). That was the year that Catholic Queen Mary was succeeded by Protestant Queen Elizabeth. In the puritanical period that followed, churches were stripped of their rood lofts and other features that were deemed to be 'popish' or overly decorative. Yet more damage was done, centuries later, by the restorations of well-meaning Victorians. It was probably Hubberholme's relative isolation that saved the church from both these fates.

Despite the church's antiquity, the pews and choir stalls are relatively modern. I remember, as a kid, being told to search for the church mice. A little carved mouse was the 'signature' of Robert Thompson, the well-known carpenter from Kilburn. Some were in out-of-the-way places, though, and could only be found by inquisitive fingers. Why a mouse? Well, the story suggests that during a church assignment, one of Thompson's fellow carvers made a comment about them being as poor as church mice. On the spur of the moment Thompson carved one. Recognising it as the ideal trademark, no finished pieces have subsequently left the workshop without featuring that little mouse.

From Hubberholme the Dales Way hugs the River Wharfe up Langstrothdale (don't you just love those names!), but I decided to make a short detour to visit one of my favourite buildings in the Dales. A track rising steeply from behind Hubberholme church brought me to the splendid façade of Scar House. This substantial house sits beneath the limestone scar that provided its name, and enjoys wonderful views across the valley. Apologies for sounding like an estate agent's blurb, but Scar House is my idea of a house. I'd buy it like a shot if I had to launder the money from a once-in-a-lifetime crack cocaine deal, and needed to keep my head down for a spell. Unfortunately – for me, at least – Scar House is not for sale.

The last time it *was* for sale, in 1989, the National Trust snapped it up. The house became their fourteenth letting cottage; now they have hundreds, and anyone can rent Scar House for a week's holiday. They'll still need a few bob, though, as it's towards the top end of the National Trust's tariff. The Yorkshire Dales are full of picturesque cottages, and, while many of them do indeed have roses round the door, they tend to be small. Cosy, no doubt, but still small. Scar House is different: the sort of place where you can lose yourself.

I've stayed here twice. The first time was almost twenty-five years ago, when the house was still in private hands. Two couples and four kids arrived to spend a long winter weekend of rest and recreation at Scar House. My kids were small. Well, one was small, the other was tiny: just a babe in arms. We had food, wine and – best of all – a huge Scalextric set.

We woke up the following morning to find ourselves snowed in. It's not unusual to get snow at this height; Scar House is, after all, 1100 feet above sea level. But this snowfall was spectacular. There was no way we could drive back down the track. We couldn't find the track. The snow had drifted so deep that we couldn't even find the cars. Plans to stay just for the weekend were jettisoned: with the children so tiny, we decided to stay at Scar House until the snow melted.

Cocooned by stowering snow against the outside world, we cranked up the heating, cracked open the wine and played Scalextric. We replicated – in miniature, but in real time – the Le Mans twenty-four-hour endurance race. We 'sledged' down the hill behind the house on some blue fertilizer bags we found in an outhouse. Each day one of us did a convincing impression of Good King Wenceslas, trudging down that long, winding track to The George and returning (though maybe not straight away) with supplies. Whenever conversation flagged, we just opened another bottle of wine. Not such a great privation, then.

Scar House dates from the middle of the sixteenth century. When the façade was rebuilt in the nineteenth century, an earlier datestone from 1698 was thoughtfully preserved in the fabric of the building. George Fox, the founder of the Quakers, stayed at Scar House in 1642, when it was the home of James Tennant and his wife Sarah. Fox recorded the occasion in his journal:

As I travelled through the Dales I came to a man's house whose name was Tennant. I was moved to speak to the family and declare God's ever-

lasting truth to them; and as I was turning away from them I was moved to turn again and speak to the man himself; and he was convinced, and his family, and lived and died in the truth.

At a time when Quakers were being persecuted for their beliefs, Scar House became one of their meeting houses. James Tennant knew the consequences of becoming a Quaker, and spent the last few years of his life imprisoned in York Castle. After his death, in 1674, his body was brought back to Scar House, and buried in the small strip of land alongside the farmhouse which served as a Quaker burial ground. His family carved the date and his initials – JT – on a large headstone (Quakers have never gone in for elaborate epitaphs). At a later date this stone was brought inside the house, where it served as a shelf in the larder. Amazingly, and evocatively, the stone is still there.

George Fox visited Scar House again, in 1677, by which time it had become the centre for Quakers from the surrounding dales, including Littondale and Bishopdale. The Toleration Act of 1689 gave Nonconformists the right to worship in the manner of their choosing. Quakers no longer had to gather in secret. By the early-eighteenth century the meetings had transferred down the dale, to Starbotton. A century later the Wharfedale Quakers had become absorbed into the Aysgarth meeting, and there are no records beyond this date of Quakers at Scar House. An inscribed plaque near the entrance to the burial ground only dates back to the 1920s when a group of Quakers – including Arthur Raistrick, the renowned Dales historian – put it there.

Yes, I love Scar House, and left it with a sigh. The grassy path leading away from it afforded good views down into the valley of Langstrothdale. Soon I came to the hamlet of Yockenthwaite. If 'hamlet' sounds a trifle archaic, is there a word that better describes a settlement comprising just three farms, a collection of outbuildings and a beautiful little packhorse bridge?

In Langstrothdale the infant River Wharfe burbles happily over little limestone ledges. When it's not in spate, you can pick your way across with a hop, skip and a jump, without even getting your feet wet. The river bank is grassy, making this the ideal place to lay out a picnic rug and doze in the sunshine. Chicken legs, some salad, maybe a glass or two of Blue Nun... while the kids paddle in the shallows. Langstrothdale is idyllic in summer; even on a chilly October day it was magical.

The Ordnance Survey map shows a stone circle here, though it's distinctly underwhelming in the flesh. It consists of twenty limestone blocks, and is thought to date to around 2200–1400BC. It's not the sort of place where you can imagine Druids dancing, or sacrificing virgins. It's the sort of stone circle you can imagine a bunch of half-cut Druids knocking up after the pubs had shut.

There is more utter tosh written about standing stones than any other feature of the landscape. For whatever reason they were built, they now act as magnets for every dope fiend who can hold a pencil-stub. Perhaps the truth is out there. Maybe stone circles *were* landing sites for extra-terrestrial space craft. But don't put your shirt on it.

It's strange. Once they dispense with regulation, bog-standard, vanilla flavoured, one-size-fits-all religion – in the shape of the Church of England – people don't hold their hands up and say: 'That's it. No more superstition and mumbo-jumbo for me. It's scientific rationality from now on.' Oh no, they're more likely to wander off into cloud-cuckoo-land, a place where the gullible and the 'hard of thinking' can feel at home. A place where new-age nonsense (astrology, tarot cards and feng shui spring to mind) is unaccountably given credence, instead of being greeted with the mocking laughter it deserves. Yes, once you loosen the constraints of common sense, anything – no matter how daft – seems possible.

They'll take some of the Bible's more outlandish statements with a pinch of salt ('Methuselah lived to be 969? Don't make me laugh') and dismiss Biblical miracles as unfeasible ('Water into wine? I don't think so. Jesus just turned wine into *vinegar* – that's what *happens* when you leave the cork out of the bottle'). But then they go and spoil it all with excitable talk of UFOs and little green men.

I've visited a few 'sacred site' sites on the internet, which range from the scholarly (but dull) to the barmy (and correspondingly entertaining). The new-age archaeologists of cyberspace begin their investigations by dropping a tab of acid, and then amaze themselves by what they see: stones that pulsate with colour, weird lights in the sky, cows that flutter their eyebrows winningly and whisper: 'Come on, Frank, you know you want it as much as I do.'

I wanted the Yockenthwaite stones to be crackling with Neolithic energy, really I did, but to me they just looked inert. Perhaps my imagination wasn't up to the task. Or maybe I just needed to take more Class A drugs. My own feeling is that every place is sacred... or no place is.

I walked beside the unenclosed road, still following the river. I passed Beckermonds, 'the meeting of the becks'. This is another compact collection of farms, situated where the Wharfe is fed by Greenfield Beck. I continued on to even smaller Oughtershaw; here I left the Hawes road and joined a good track following Oughtershaw Beck. A sign reassured me that Cam Houses – my immediate destination – was just 2½ miles away. This was unfamiliar territory for me and – in retrospect, at least – where the Dales Way stopped being an undemanding riverside ramble.

I found myself entering a long, expansive valley, as lonely and empty as any in the Dales. It hasn't even got a name. You could call it either an Area of Outstanding Natural Beauty (AONB), or an Awful Lot of Bugger-All (ALBA), depending on your mood, the time of year and the prevailing weather. I passed a lonely farm called Nethergill, then an even lonelier one called Swarthgill. It was here that a little dog – like a loo brush on legs – dashed out and nipped me on the ankle.

I saw another sign to Cam Houses, only there seemed to have been a recount. Despite having walked a couple of miles since the last sign, I found the distance had been rounded up to 3 miles. Alice in Wonderland might have understood, but not me. Beyond Swarthgill the track degenerated into a boggy, peaty path, which slowed my progress. And, just for good measure, it started to rain. At that particular moment, civilisation seemed a long way away. If I was to twist an ankle here, no one would find me. I would punch numbers into my mobile phone, to no effect whatsoever, cursing Richard Bleeding Branson with my dying breath. I would eventually be identified from that useless phone, still clutched in a skeletal hand. Who would miss me, anyway? Well, for a start, there would be all my creditors, my immediate family, and a close circle of nodding acquaintances and drinking buddies. I'm a popular guy. And if I had any friends, they would tell you the same.

The landscape hereabouts was bleak yet beautiful. I wished I had more time to stand and enjoy the view, but my legs were tired and my boots were picking up great clouts of mud with every sodden step. In drizzle, with the late afternoon light fading, I was very glad to sight Cam Houses in the distance: a couple of the highest and most isolated dwellings in the Dales.

This was the Pennine watershed. With laboured bounds I jumped a couple of tiny becks. One of them would become the Wharfe, flowing 75 delectable miles through the Dales to Cawood, where it merges with the waters of the Swale, Ure and Nidd to become the River Ouse, which decants, via the Humber Estuary, into the North Sea. The other beck, rising just a few yards further on, would become the River Ribble and flow across the plain of Lancashire to meet the Irish Sea. For reasons I'm still not too sure about, I find this utterly amazing.

The views were magnificent in all directions, but I was more conscious of the rain, my aching feet and the fading light. As I approached lonely Cam Houses, I felt I couldn't take another step. So it stopped me in my tracks to find the place deserted, and the bunk-barn closed. Here I was, miles from anywhere; I had nowhere to sleep and it was getting dark. I cursed my fate, I cursed whoever it was who'd told me I would find a warm welcome at Cam House bunk-barn, and I cursed Richard Branson again… just out of habit.

There was no option but to keep on walking. Ingleborough loomed large ahead – wearing not so much a cap of cloud, but what looked like a ten-gallon hat. Passing a gloomy plantation of conifers, I joined Cam High Road, a track that was already old by the time the Romans improved it. The road linked the Roman forts of Bainbridge and Ribchester, and remained a busy highway until the turnpike road from Hawes to Ingleton was built. I passed a cairn that confirmed this as the highest point of the Dales Way, at 1700 feet. For a mile the Dales Way and the Pennine Way shared the ruler-straight Roman road… not that I saw another living soul. I stumbled down this rocky track, into the Ribblehead valley. Thank God I'd bought a torch; this God-forsaken spot was no place to be at nightfall. Ghostly dogs roamed this wasteland, their red eyes as big as, oh, dinner plates probably.

Unlikely as it may seem to anyone who is familiar with the area, at that particular moment Ribblehead represented 'civilisation.' As night descended I pinned my hopes on the lights of the Station Inn that twinkled way down in the valley. I decided this was my destination for the night. There was nowhere else to go. If they wanted to get rid of me at closing time they'd have to throw me out, because I'd be clinging to the door jambs with my fingertips and shrieking like a girl.

I met tarmac near Gearstones Farm, once an inn that catered for the drovers and packhorse men. There must have been some wild old nights out here: no need to worry about waking the neighbours. I trudged along the road to the Station Inn which, unsurprisingly, is opposite Ribblehead Station on the celebrated Settle–Carlisle railway line.

I staggered inside and buttonholed the landlord. 'You'll have a room for me,' I said, trying to make it sound more like a statement than a question. He looked doubtful: 'I've got the RAF staying here tonight.' 'What, *all* of them?' I remember saying… indicating that my brain was as befuddled as my legs were weary. He glanced at the ledger again, smiled, and found there was a room free after all. He won't remember that moment; I was just another weary rambler. But I will.

I sat back and relaxed – happy to be out of the rain, and in from the all-pervading dark. It's amazing how quickly your mood can change once you have a pint in your hand and a lady slides a hot meal under your nose. I eavesdropped on the cheerfully inconsequential conversations around me. It's written into the constitution that everyone has the right to go into the pub of his or her choice and talk absolute bollocks. And the customers of the Station Inn were exercising that ancient right with infectious enthusiasm.

Someone fed the jukebox, encouraging Meatloaf to sing one of his more baffling numbers: 'I Will do Anything for Love, but I Won't do That'. After a couple of pints, it got me thinking. What is it, exactly, that Meatloaf was so squeamish about? Was it some sexual peccadillo so unhygienic that he just couldn't bring himself to sing about it? Was it something so embarrassing – to do with his weight, perhaps – that he didn't want to share with the world?

And that can't be his real name, surely. I bet it's a nickname from school; children can be so cruel, can't they? What would you call him if you met him? Mr Loaf? Or Meat, perhaps, once you'd got to know him a little better. A lot of people think of him as just another fat pomp-rocker with lank, greasy hair. But his music will live on, as long as people listen to overwrought love songs. I mean, listen to the guy: 'I'll do anything for love.' Well, except for *that*, of course.

These are the kind of witless thoughts that waft around a man's empty head, when he's tired, footsore and his brain has already started to shut down operations for the night. Once I got to my bed, I slept like I'd been clubbed on the head.

Day Five

RIBBLEHEAD TO SEDBERGH

Ribblehead Viaduct

Ribblehead is, at first sight, an awful lot of precious little: one of the areas that the authors of the Domesday Book wrote off, dismissively, as 'waste'. But appearances can be deceptive, and the more you look around you, the more there is to see.

The main attractions, of course, are the Three Peaks: Ingleborough, Whernside and the Welsh-sounding Pen-y-ghent (it means 'the windy hill', apparently). Ingleborough and Pen-y-ghent are familiar landmarks; those who know the Dales will be able to recognise these hills from their distinctive silhouettes alone. Whernside, though the least impressive to look at, is the highest of the trio – in fact, the highest hill in Yorkshire – at 2415 feet.

The Three Peaks are sufficiently close to be considered in the same breath, yet sufficiently distant to provide a challenge for walkers and runners. The Three Peaks challenge walk covers a demanding 24 miles, and the challenge is to complete it inside twelve hours. Peak-baggers traditionally clock in and out at the walkers' café in Horton-in-Ribblesdale, which makes a convenient start and finish point. Fit walkers take eight or nine hours to complete the challenge. Fell runners have been known to do it in two and a half hours; just thinking about that makes me want to have a little lie-down.

The walk is popular. *Too* popular. Countless pairs of walking boots have etched the footpaths deeply into the hillsides. Whenever they encounter a boggy bit, walkers tend to walk around. It's human nature – we've all done it – but all it does is broaden these paths even more. The erosion is exacerbated by the high rainfall and poor drainage. Despite the fact that there are dozens of walks in the Dales that are as good, or better, the Three Peaks have taken quite a pounding over the years. Something had to be done.

The paths have been repaired and consolidated over the years, with a variety of materials. Wooden duckboards were laid over the peat bogs; they kept walkers' boots dry, but were ugly and intrusive. More recent methods – such as stone-flagged causeways and artfully constructed steps – are arguably more 'natural'. With the passing of the years these improvements will no doubt blend into the landscape. Walkers will continue to debate the merit of these measures, heatedly, for as long as the pub landlords of the Dales will serve them beer. From my own perspective the fault seems to lie, once again, with the 80 per cent of the people who visit just 20 per cent of the places.

Ribblehead is limestone country *par excellence*, riddled with caves, limestone outcrops and lush ravines filled with rowan trees, rare flowers and tumbling water. You can find Roman roads, old packhorse bridges and a hot dog and hamburger stand called, sensibly enough, The Fourth Peak.

I love the limestone scenery. But to get me down a pothole, you'd have to put a loaded gun to my head. And I still wouldn't do it. If mountain climbing fuels my fear of falling off and hurting myself (not an irrational fear at all, in my opinion), then potholing awakens deeper, more primeval terrors. I combat these terrors in the best possible way, by trying to avoid them altogether. There are plenty of people who are happy to spend their weekends crawling on their bellies into the bowels of the earth; they don't need me to join them.

Those of us without proper training, equipment or 'bottle' should stay well clear of these limestone caves. But to cater for those who want the experience, without all the hard work, there are two or three occasions each year when visitors are winched down into Gaping Gill, near Ingleborough. They make a sweaty-palmed descent of 350 feet into a chamber so vast that it could accommodate York Minster. I'm not sure what the Dean of York would have to say about that. But surely it's worth a try.

The official Dales Way includes some road walking hereabouts, so I decided to begin Day Five with another detour: a high-level route 'over the tops'. From the Station Inn I wandered down to the Ribblehead Viaduct: probably the finest example of railway engineering on the Settle–Carlisle line, and certainly the longest of its viaducts. This is a wild and windswept place. In the good old days – when steam trains laboured across the viaduct, and fact and fantasy were as one – the wind could blow the coal right off the fireman's shovel. On one occasion an engine driver's cap was snatched from his head; it was blown underneath an arch of the viaduct before landing back on his head again. It's true – as true as I'm standing here talking bollocks.

The Settle–Carlisle line was a railway built on bluff and brinkmanship; cold logic suggests it should never have been built at all. It certainly wouldn't be built today; we simply couldn't afford it. With the politics of prevarication that hold sway, especially when transport issues are concerned, I doubt if any government could take a decision whose ramifications extended beyond the next election.

Back in 1860, though, when railway mania held the country in its grip, the Midland Railway Company was trying to expand its operations from London to the North. The Midland ran trains as far as Ingleton; travellers going further north had to change track and use trains that belonged to a rival outfit, the London & North-Western Railway. Passengers had to make an undignified dash through Ingleton to board their 'connecting' train. But such was the low priority given by the LNWR to Midland travellers that all too often they would be greeted by the sight of their train disappearing into the distance. And the LNWR wouldn't let the Midland run trains on their track.

Strange how history repeats itself. Fast forward 140 odd years to the present day. Yes, anyone who has had the misfortune to travel by train since privatisation will recognise this depressing scenario.

But I digress... James Allport, general manager of the Midland Railway Company, became as frustrated as his customers. What the company needed was a new route to Carlisle that would cut out the need to use LNWR trains at all. Railway engineers had already discounted the idea of a direct route to Carlisle, because of the hilly Pennine terrain. Nevertheless that is exactly what Mr Allport proposed when the company placed a bill before Parliament.

By the time the bill was passed, in 1866, the company was having second thoughts. The bill might even have been nothing more than an audacious bluff, to persuade the LNWR to be more co-operative. If it *was* a bluff, it proved to be a very expensive one – since Parliament insisted that the line should indeed go ahead.

An army of navvies was mustered in 1869 to built this most improbable of railways. They laboured with pick and shovel; it was hard slog all the way. The only labour-saving device was the one that had been recently discovered by Alfred Nobel; the longest tunnel on the line, at 2629 yards, was driven through the bleakness of Blea Moor with dynamite.

The easier route for the railway would have been along the valley bottoms. But Mr Allport didn't want to build another branch line, with trains pootling from station to station; he wanted his passengers to travel in 100mph express trains. It was to be the Victorian equivalent of a motorway. The challenge was to make the route as straight as possible, while keeping gradients acceptably shallow. Because of this uncompromising attitude, a total of 14 tunnels and 21 viaducts were needed. The enterprise proved far more expensive than had been envisaged. The bill totalled £3.5 million – a staggering sum at the time – rather than the £2 million that had been estimated. That's another statistic that will have the rail passengers of the twenty-first century nodding their heads in weary recognition.

Of all the terrain between Settle and Carlisle, Ribblehead proved to be the most inhospitable, not least because of the weather. Ribblehead has the dubious distinction of holding the Yorkshire record for rainfall: 190 inches fell in 1954, compared to a national average of about 70 inches.

Two major engineering projects were undertaken at Ribblehead. The navvies had to drive Blea Moor tunnel through these Pennine hills, and raise the 24 arches of Ribblehead Viaduct. Have you ever wondered how the viaduct was built? No, me neither... but it's fascinating anyway. Old photographs give the secret away. A wooden superstructure was constructed, to create what was essentially a viaduct in negative, around which the stone-built pillars were erected. The wooden scaffolding was rounded at the top, so that the stonework could be continued into the correct arched shapes. At the completion of each section, the scaffolding was dismantled, and re-erected further on.

So many navvies were needed for the task – perhaps as many as 2000 – that they lived on-site. Shanty towns grew up all along the route of the Settle–Carlisle, bearing such fanciful names as Sebastapol, Inkerman, Jerusalem and Jericho – with echoes of both the Crimean War and the Old Testament. While the viaduct and tunnel were being built, there was a shanty town at Ribblehead known as Batty Green. It was, by all accounts, like a frontier town from the Wild West: a lawless, drunken place were a man once sold his wife for the price of a barrel of beer (and reckoned to have got the best of the bargain).

Life was cheap in other ways too, and many navvies died – most through accidents at work, a few from bar brawls. To add to the misery, other lives were claimed by an outbreak of smallpox in 1871. The 200 men, women and children who lost their lives while building the railway were buried in the graveyard of the little church of St Leonard, 2 miles down the road, in secluded Chapel-le-Dale. Inside the church is their memorial.

The allure of steam trains is something that has passed me by. It used to worry me. After all, a man who doesn't get turned on when he sees steam escaping from a cast-iron boiler (and who, incidentally, watches football matches purely for their aesthetic qualities) might just as well go the whole hog and take up ballet.

With so much interest these days in the Settle–Carlisle railway line – from steam-train buffs and sane people alike – it's difficult to appreciate just how close the line came, during the 1980s, to being closed down. British Rail, as it was then, operated a policy of 'closure by stealth'. This took the form of running fewer trains, and failing to make vital repairs to the fabric of the line – hoping to make the service so user-unfriendly that travellers would make alternative arrangements. Then British Rail would triumphantly display a graph of declining passenger numbers, and thereby fulfill their mission statement: to run a once-great railway system into the ground. It is an overly familiar ploy.

If 'closure by stealth' meant that no one would notice, then British Rail got their timing wrong. An army of rail enthusiasts banded together and kicked up such a fuss that (I'm cutting a long story short here, because I'm getting bored) the Settle–Carlisle line won a reprieve. Hooray! The best way to ensure the future of the line is to use it. So be sure to take a trip on the Settle–Carlisle line at the next opportunity. Have a day out in Carlisle, enjoy a walk in limestone country or take one of the steam-hauled 'specials' that are laid on by train enthusiasts. You may have to share your sandwiches with some bearded loon whose conversation extends no further than the number of bogies on the carriage and the engine driver's middle name, but that's a small price to pay if it helps to keep the trains running.

Ah, steam-train buffs. It's all too easy, isn't it, to mock an interest that we ourselves don't happen to share. So let's have a go...

Years ago, when the Yorkshire Dales weren't as familiar to me as they are today, a steam train buff invited me to spend a day 'up the Dales,' photographing an old puffer on the Settle–Carlisle line. It seemed like a good idea at the time. A sunny Saturday morning found us filling up the car with enough photographic equipment to stock a small shop, and heading north. Armed with a rail timetable Dave knew just where to go to get the best shots. The first port of call was an old railway bridge that offered an uninterrupted view down a valley, along which this particular steam train (it had a name, but I've forgotten it) was to come.

It wasn't just Dave who had earmarked this bridge as the perfect vantage point; on arrival there were dozens of photographers setting up an arsenal of matt-black gadgetry. There were one or two undemanding souls armed with only a couple of cameras and a bag full of lenses, but the real diehards scorned such a miserly approach. One fellow set up five separate tripods, each sporting a camera and motor-drive. His lenses ranged from fish-eye to a bazooka-sized monster that could take a characterful head-and-shoulders portrait of an ant at a thousand paces. And how did he hope to fire all these cameras? No problem: remote releases fitted with air-bulbs. He held one in each hand, one beneath each foot, and the fifth clenched between his teeth. I kid you not. He may have looked like the protagonist of some medieval torture, but there was no way that he was going to miss the decisive moment.

My own desire to record this particular steam train on film was fading by the minute, as video cameras and tape recorders made their appearance. Every square foot of available space on the bridge was filled with expectant photographers. Film was loaded, lenses prefocused, shutters cocked, apertures set, tape rewound... as the climactic moment approached. Yes, there it was: in the distance an undistinguished steam loco begin its laboured ascent.

It was at this moment that a young fellow – armed only with a little 'point & shoot' camera – ran down to the trackside and took up a position between the massed ranks of photographers and the approaching train. Standing there with the camera to his eye he was an uninvited guest in everyone else's viewfinders.

An anguished voice broke the astonished silence. 'Excuse me,' it said, 'you're in the way; can you please move?' Only it wasn't in so many words. The interloper cast a myopic glance backwards, shrugged his shoulders and stood his ground. The voice was joined by others: an enraged chorus threatening him with grievous bodily harm if he didn't shift. The fellow's response, a V-sign, sealed his fate; a dozen photographers scrambled down to the trackside and proceeded to sort him out.

But the train had arrived... with great billows of smoke and a good head of steam. For a few seconds, before we on the bridge were engulfed in steam and smoke, the clicking of camera shutters was deafening. Hundreds of pictures were 'in the can' – each and every composition enlivened by a knot of brawling photographers in the foreground.

Without pausing for breath, everyone hurled their hardware into car boots. A posse of MOT failures was soon heading off at suicidal speeds, along narrow Dales roads, to rendezvous with the same train at the next photogenic port of call.

My first thought, after witnessing this orgy of picture taking, was regret at not having bought shares in Kodak. Then I wondered what the tape recordings must have sounded like: the random percussion of camera shutters and motor-drives, the screams of photographers attacking one another, and what's that noise in the background? Oh yes, it's a steam train...

Don't get me wrong; I've nothing against people who photograph old steam trains. No doubt they all have mothers who love them. But count me out.

The day's walk began by accompanying the monumental arches of Ribblehead Viaduct. I followed a good track alongside the railway, up to the signal box at Blea Moor. A railwayman's pebble-dashed house occupied as desolate a site as I could imagine. I tried (but failed) to compose an upbeat description of the property, as it might appear in an estate agent's window, without resorting to the word 'God-forsaken'. Who – as Loyd Grossman would say, in those strangulated vowels of his – would live in a house like this? Well, someone who was happy with his own company, for a start – and possessed of a good memory too. Someone who wouldn't get home from a full day's expedition to the shops, only to find he'd forgotten to buy a carton of milk. I don't think any shop would deliver.

It was at this moment that the RAF (in the shape of a dozen ferociously fit squaddies) trotted past me as I was doing up a boot-lace. They were all carrying huge packs; I doubted whether they had bothered to choose between the relative merits of a torch or a mobile phone. If the choice had been between the kitchen sink and a portable anvil, it looked like they'd packed both, to be on the safe side. By the time I'd finished with my bootlace, they had disappeared over the distant horizon.

Where the railway disappears into the blackness of Blea Moor tunnel, I crossed the line on an ingenious bridge which carries both the footpath and the rushing waters of Little Dale Beck. I passed Force Gill, a waterfall that hammered over a rocky ledge. The water was peaty brown – the colour of stewed tea – like most waterfalls in the Dales, rather than the milky white water you see in Lakeland. The path got steeper. I always know when a path gets really steep, because I get the urge to stop, turn round, put hands on hips and drink in some gorgeous view. This is, of course, merely a diversionary tactic that allows me to take a few deep breaths, while not letting on to my walking companions just how unfit I am. On my own, of course, I was free to sit down on a rock until the lung-bursting gasps subsided.

I followed a sandy track up the hillside; it seemed to float over the black, venomous mud. Newly laid, the track looked a bit like the yellow-brick road from *The Wizard of Oz*, but in time it will no doubt blend more harmoniously into its surroundings. I appreciated a good track underfoot, especially when I had to negotiate unimproved sections where I sank into mud and peat up to my boot tops.

Halfway up the hill a path headed off west. This is the route that Three Peaks baggers follow, to reach the summit of Whernside. Though 'summit' seems a misnomer for the top of a hill that even its closest friends liken to a beached whale. It was at this junction that I stepped aside to allow a faster walker to get past. His speed was surprising, considering he was walking sideways in crab-fashion, bent double and clutching himself purposefully.

'You're slow,' he admonished me, cheerfully, as he came to a breathless halt. 'Well, I'm not in any particular hurry,' I said. 'Look at me,' he went on, 'I've got a groin strain. I did the Three Peaks yesterday and it's going to take more than a groin strain to stop me doing it again today.'

His expression indicated he was requesting admiration rather than the smack in the mouth he deserved. I wanted to grab his walking stick and use it to beat some sense into him. What idiocy makes a man take to the hills when by rights he should be lying on a sofa and putting his feet up? What bizarre need could drive him so pointlessly through the pain barrier towards a future swaddled in a truss?

Walking fast is a contradiction in terms, like meditating in a hurry. It makes walkers look no further ahead – for safety's sake – than the toecaps of their boots. It's not a mentality I understand; what's the point of walking if it isn't to slow down sufficiently to enjoy the sights, sounds, smells and tastes of the countryside?

They walk fast at the Olympics too. *Very* fast. And once you've watched two dozen people walking as fast as they can – in that ridiculously awkward, hip-swaying style, as they try vainly to keep at least one foot in contact with the ground at all times – you have as convincing a symbol as you could ever hope to find of the sheer futility of life. There's a word for walking fast. It's 'running'.

On my saunters in the Dales I regularly come across cagoule-clad plodders, whose joyless expressions indicate that walking has become more of a penance than a pleasure. They march stolidly, stoically, stupidly, through wind and rain, as though a masked robber had broken into their homes, held their families to ransom with a pump-action rifle and barked: 'You… yes you with the straggly beard and the gaiters… walk 20 miles through featureless peat hags… right now… or I'll blow your wife and kids away.'

For a certain breed of heads-down, no-nonsense challenge walkers, the Dales are a giant treadmill on which they can play out their morose fantasies, hoping to trim a few minutes off their personal best time for traversing one dreary tract of moorland or another. They brag, bafflingly, of miles logged… rather than views admired or pleasures experienced. They make me weak with their foolishness.

As one of life's dawdlers, I don't share their urgency. If I drove the way I walked, I would be pottering along, straddling the white line at a stately 30mph, utterly oblivious to other road users. The point about a walk is that there's nothing you have to do. Except walk. And even then you don't have to do that. It's your choice. Right, I've got my breath back now…

It was a long haul up to the top of the hill, but well worth the effort. From the highpoint of Great Wold, the views were as panoramic as anywhere in the Dales. At those times when our little island seems unbearably crowded, a view like this can provide some much-needed perspective.

People sometime talk as though our countryside was already beyond redemption. 'It's doomed, doomed,' as that wild-eyed Scottish loon used to say in 'Dad's Army'. The hedgerows are disappearing, we hear, and greedy developers keep bulldozing ancient woodlands, just so they can build another accursed out-of-town shopping complex. And, God knows, there are a lot of people who seem to dedicate themselves to leaving the countryside a little more screwed up than when they found it. It's easy to get depressed.

So we need to see the bigger picture once in a while. To stand on a rock, gaze at a such a view and reassure ourselves that this little island isn't irredeemably ruined after all. I'm not suggesting we should become complacent... but just acknowledge that we have some wonderfully diverse landscapes. They haven't all disappeared. We still have so much to celebrate. And the best protection for our treasured landscapes is for as many people as possible to love them and visit them. I find it hard to believe that anyone could stand on the top of Great Wold, drink in that view, and still feel it could be improved by a burger bar or time-share holiday complex. A decent pub, though, and a pint of Timothy Taylor's Landlord Bitter: I dunno, I might go for that.

Despite visitor numbers to the honey-pot villages and attractions, we should never dissuade people from visiting the countryside. It's good for us all, in ways we can't even imagine when we're cooped up in an office or staring vacantly at the overwhelming tide of tat and trivia on TV. We just need to juggle the numbers a bit. If 80 per cent of visitors go to just 20 per cent of the places, we have to encourage people to look a little further afield than the most obvious destinations. There's plenty of room in the Dales... if people would just spread themselves out a bit.

I found the ruins of what had probably been a shepherd's hut: the perfect place to eat one of those sticky cereal bars. I sat, stoically, like some grazing ruminant, gazing vacantly at that stunning panorama. From here the Settle–Carlisle line looked like a child's railway set, assembled in a landscape constructed from chicken wire and plaster of Paris. Looking down, I saw the track emerge from Blea Moor tunnel and cross the viaducts of Dent Head and Arten Gill. The line swept along the flanks of Wold Fell and Great Knoutberry Hill, to the windswept little station at Dent, the highest railway station in the land. And can there be another station that is so far from the community whose name it bears? Unwary travellers, stepping onto the platform, face a walk of 4 miles to Dent itself (and it feels like 8). Beyond Dent Station, snow fences protect the tracks from the worst of winter weather. And, round here, that can be severe indeed. Northbound trains disappear into Rise Hill tunnel, re-emerging in the equally bleak surroundings of Garsdale Head.

This was, in every sense, one of the high points of the Dales Way. The view wasn't one of rugged peaks or sharp silhouettes. No hills stood head and shoulders above another. These Dales hills looked more like the rounded flanks of sleeping animals. On a grey autumn day, with the wind whipping around my head, it had a sullen splendour: a sense of space, and the perfect antidote to world weariness and other twenty-first century ills.

I had the landscape to myself until I came across a bunch of puzzled teenagers, holding their maps first one way and then another. The group leader said they were looking for a contour line. I said I was pretty sure I'd seen one that very morning, and bid them farewell.

As I followed an old thoroughfare – the Craven Way – another wonderful vista opened up ahead. Dentdale looked impossibly green (this was late October, remember), with hedgerows as well as dry-stone walls to divide the pasture up into neat little fields. The Craven Way became stonier and boggier as it descended into the valley. It was a relief to join a metalled road; I accompanied first Deepdale Beck, then the delectable River Dee on a raised floodbank.

The river delivered me to Dent, another of my favourite places. It has managed to remain unspoiled without becoming too twee. Being tucked away in its own little dale has helped; Dent is not really on the way to anywhere. Most through traffic takes the A684 through Garsdale, a few miles to the north, which is the only A-road to cross the National Park from east to west. It's for the best: a tractor and half a dozen cars would comprise a major traffic jam in Dent.

With its narrow, cobbled streets, and stone houses clustered in a horseshoe shape around the church, Dent feels like a Dales village. But the houses are nearly all whitewashed, and that's more typical of the Lake District. Dent Town, to give the place its Sunday-best name, has a self-contained air, as befitting its isolated situation. A few generations back, the main industry was hand-knitting. But the last big job was knitting scarves for 'Doctor Who'; once the series was cancelled, the work just seemed to dry up. Some of the older houses had first-floor galleries, open to the elements, where the knitters would sit, but the galleries and their nimble-fingered occupants are all gone.

In the middle of Dent is the Sedgwick Monument, a slab of Shap granite that incorporates a drinking fountain. It commemorates Adam Sedgwick, a local man whose father had been the vicar of Dent for more than fifty years. After studying at Sedbergh School, Adam went on to become Professor of Geology at Cambridge University. He was another Dalesman who never forgot his birthplace; much of what we know of this isolated dale – and not just the geology – came from his pen.

After a second restorative pint at the Sun Inn (I'd managed to spill the first one over the carpet, due to dwindling hand/eye/mouth co-ordination), I continued along the River Dee through Dentdale. The next few miles were a bit of a blur, frankly. I trudged joylessly through the increasingly sodden landscape in that impassive, head-down way that I'd noticed long-distance walkers adopt. Yes, the puritan walk ethic was kicking in. Only a fool would carry on walking through driving rain. I pulled my hood of my cagoule tighter around my face, and carried on.

I approached another walker. In a moment that readers of *Animal Farm* would instantly recognise, I looked at him, he looked at me… and there was nothing to choose between us. Just another pair of sodden hikers who had lost the plot.

I was tired and hungry; my feet ached. Nevertheless, there was a grim satisfaction from plodding along. I kept walking because, by now, it just seemed to be what I did. Like Magnus Magnusson, I'd started, so I'd finish. I trudged through narrow lanes lined with moss-covered walls, that already had a Lakeland 'feel' and smell. When you're walking on roads, the usual advice is to keep to the right; it means you can see the oncoming traffic. But I decided to walk on the left. If I was going to be mown down by a speeding car, on such a wet and miserable day, I'd rather not know about it. The rain pattered down through the trees, my feet scuffed through the leaves on the road, and my waterproof over-trousers scrunched together loudly, like someone in the seat behind you at the cinema who's fondling a bag of cheese and onion crisps.

At some point I left the Dee, to accompany the River Rawthey, but I really can't remember where. One river was beginning to look very much like another. As the rain hammered down, I came to the inescapable conclusion that the enjoyment had stopped a few miles back down the track. So, naturally enough, it seemed to take an age to get to Sedbergh, where I'd planned to stay the night. As a pick-me-up, I promised myself a night out in the big city. To see Sedbergh as a bustling metropolis, it helps if you've spent the previous few hours staggering about in heavy rain.

Sedbergh is the largest town within the Yorkshire Dales National Park, though since the boundary wiggles to exclude towns such as Skipton, Settle and Richmond, this isn't saying a great deal. It was the boundary change of 1974 that ceded Sedbergh from West Yorkshire to Cumbria. And, for once, the change made sense.

Most people will probably associate Sedbergh with the boys' public school, which was founded way back in 1525. It was traditional for well-heeled parents to pack off their sons to a boys-only school miles from anywhere (and, Lord love us, it still is). Places where maladjusted older guys – otherwise known as teachers – could fraternise with impressionable young lads during their hormone-fuelled years of puberty, when there was so much testosterone around, they could actually hear it popping (it sounds like idle fingers fondling bubblewrap).

I am reliably informed by an ex-pupil (thanks for the memories, John) that Sedbergh School used to be a hotbed of buggery. But there was a downside to public school too. In fair weather or foul, small boys dressed only in shorts and vests were forced to run up and down the Howgill Fells that form a backcloth to the town. It was 'character building' apparently. Those that survived this punishing regime got a good grounding for a career in the diplomatic service or merchant banking or maybe a theatrical drag-act.

As with so many of our foremost public schools, Sedbergh placed great emphasis on sporting achievement. Boys would cheer on the school's football team with a song that conjured up the landscape. It went: 'The sunshine is melting the snow on the Calf, and the Rawthay is loud in the Dale', and it was sung to the tune of that lovely old ballad: 'We're gonna fuckin' kill ya.'

My mate John still bears the scars from his years at Sedbergh School: mostly psychological, plus the occasional groin strain. It's all different now, of course; buggery is probably just an extra-curricular option, like art or music. But I only have to mention Battenburg cake, apple-pie beds and wanking contests and he gets all misty-eyed with nostalgia.

I staggered into a hotel, and got myself a room. Soaked and muddy, I must have been an unprepossessing sight. God knows why they let me in through the door. After a restorative bath, I hit the nightspots. When it comes to idle recreation, I am endlessly optimistic. Despite all evidence to the contrary, I look forward to an enjoyable evening. I fantasise that I have all the social skills necessary to orchestrate a pleasant few hours – whether it's sharing jokes around the bar, thrashing the locals at pool or flirting outrageously with a barmaid who's thinking, 'Bloody hell, he's gorgeous.' But it seldom pans out that way. I don't know why.

At the risk of offending those who love the place, I can confidently say that a wet Tuesday night in Sedbergh was about as much fun as having a boil lanced. The first pub I tried was quiet. A few locals stood at the bar – sucking their teeth, studying the backs of their hands with exaggerated interest – waiting for something, anything, to happen. The landlord wiped a greasy cloth across the bar, and checked his watch. It was like time had stood still. He shook his watch and held it to his ear. Then he checked his pulse, discreetly, and gave a sigh of weary resignation.

Sitting at a table, an ill-matched couple presented a convincing picture of mutual indifference. He stared at the point where the wall meets the ceiling, while her mouth was set in a grim rictus that spoke – wordlessly yet eloquently – of a marriage filled with sexual disappointment. In the game of love they were just playing out extra time, waiting for the final whistle to blow.

A fake fire flickered unconvincingly; like the burning bush in the Bible, it blazed but was not consumed. You could have tossed an empty fag packet on the fire, and it would have still been there when the landlord turned the fire off at closing time, with a contemptuous flick of a switch.

Through an alcove I could see an old guy; he was sitting on his own in the next room. He looked immeasurably sad and lonely, staring gloomily into the bottom of an empty beer glass. It actually cheered me up momentarily – on the basis that someone could look worse than I felt – but only until I realised it wasn't an alcove at all… but a mirror. And that sad old geezer in the corner was, of course, me.

I didn't give up. Not me. I tried a couple of other pubs, but they only made the first one seem lively by comparison. Then, just as I was wondering if 8.30pm was too early to go to bed, I heard a noise I'd never heard before. It was my mobile phone ringing, with a loving voice at the other end and welcome news from home. Oh, thank you, Mr Branson, thank you…

Day Six

SEDBERGH TO KENDAL

Brigflatts Meeting House

Hotels – even small ones – seem to compete with each other to see which establishment can create the most anodyne atmosphere. I'm not suggesting that every room should have a different theme, like some Las Vegas honeymoon suite. But a little imagination wouldn't go amiss. My room seemed drearily familiar: floral wallpaper, electric kettle, tea bags, tiny plastic pots of long-life milk (impossible to open, unpleasant to drink), shower cap, individually wrapped bars of soap, folder of tourist brochures, TV mounted high up on the wall, and prints of insipid watercolour paintings. If these amenities are supposed to make customers feel at home, then they only emphasise how far they are from home.

Finding a Gideons' Bible in a bedside drawer, I did what anybody else would have done: I read a few improving verses of the Epistles to the Ephesians, before going downstairs for breakfast. The other guests whispered in conspiratorial huddles, as though they were making plans to rob Sedbergh's Post Office instead of just walking the Howgills. The clatter of cutlery, by contrast, seemed deafening, as they tried to scrape the pattern off the plates. Yes, it's a noisy world we live in. And when breakfast cereals are actually being promoted by the amount of din they make, you just know we're all halfway to the madhouse. I declined the snap, crackle and pop; the Weetabix in my bowl was silent and supine, soaking up milk like a bath sponge. It tasted like papier mâché. I tore the sachets of sugar open, unwrapped the pats of butter and ripped the lids off tiny tubs of marmalade – glad to have something to occupy my hands and lessen the embarrassment of sharing my first meal of the day with total strangers.

It was a blustery morning. The leaves weren't falling decorously to the ground; they were being ripped from the branches by a gusting wind. Without much enthusiasm I hoisted the rucksack onto my shoulders and headed west out of Sedbergh, along the cobbled main street. I passed the auction mart, where a couple of wet farmers were counting wet sheep into pens. It's a job that needs two men, apparently: one to say 'Yan, tan, tethera', and the other to keep prodding him awake.

Farmers, eh? We hardly know what to think of them these days. Their standing in the community rises and falls like an overheated stock market, as new and terrible afflictions are laid at their door. We know where we are with estate agents and solicitors: bottom-feeding creatures that only their mothers could love. But farmers go from hero to villain and back again – not in a generation, but in a matter of weeks. One minute they're rosy-cheeked custodians of the countryside; then, suddenly, they're damned as greedy opportunists who spend their time grubbing up hedgerows and banking subsidy cheques.

Farmers are unsentimental (or 'realistic,' if you prefer) about their livestock. A lot of townies are surprised to learn that farmers don't have a pet name for every sheep and dairy cow. Farming bears little relationship to what they may have read in The Ladybird Book of Farming. It's barbarous, brutal, dog-eat-dog... like pensioners at a jumble sale. It's easy to blame farmers for BSE, CJD, E-Coli: the whole alphabet soup of livestock mismanagement. But how were they to know that changing their livestock from herbivores into carnivores (by feeding diseased carcasses to cattle) would create so many problems in the food chain?

I've read somewhere that the hill farmers of the North of England are to the Labour Government what the miners were to the Tories. Which, judging from recent history, is not good news for the hill farmers of the North of England. But farming isn't like other jobs at all. You can't put a hill farm on a three-day week, or close down operations until the economy picks up. You can't tell the cows they won't be fed or milked till a week on Friday. It's a seven-day-a-week kind of life, for fifty-two weeks of the year (except maybe a couple of days off each year to attend Smithfield Show or a seminar about bulls' semen).

Being a hill farmer was bad enough before the foot and mouth epidemic swept across the country like one of the plagues of old Egypt. Pennine farmers couldn't sell their sheep. Prices at auction were so low that it wasn't worth taking sheep to market. On a few well-publicised occasions, sheep were being handed in to the RSPCA. This glut in the meat market led to lamb cutlets being sold by the supermarkets for a price of just 20p per kilo (just kidding).

And now, *after* foot and mouth, hill farming is looking damn-near impossible. Politicians suggest, glibly, that hill farmers should diversify. But that's easier said than done. You try telling these guys to run a petting zoo or sell premium foods over the internet. The hill farmers' usual response, when faced with adversity, is to work harder. Hard work is their currency. The farming community has its own skewed internal logic, and a deeply conservative nature that abhors change. But if a man can't make a living by working sixty hours a week, what's the point of him working eighty?

Hill farmers hang on as long as they can. Selling the farm is the last resort. It must be crushing to be the one who has to bring a family's farming dynasty to an inglorious end, with the finality of an on-site auction held under grey and gloomy skies. It's not a decision to be taken lightly. If there is a small silver lining on this big, black cloud, it's that a few farmers will be able to quit the business without losing too much face with their neighbours.

The hill farmers of the Yorkshire Dales are an endangered species. In twenty years time we'll be wondering not why hill farming declined so quickly, but how come it lasted so long.

Within a few minutes I was taking the narrow lane leading into the tiny community of Brigflatts – once noted for flax weaving. Here can be found another of my favourite buildings. The Quaker Meeting House is small, plain, unpretentious and imbued with a silence and a spirituality that is almost tangible. Almost everything I'm not, in fact.

Big isn't necessarily better, especially when we're talking about churches and chapels. York Minster, for example, is huge, awe-inspiring and magnificent: a building of architectural superlatives. But somehow – and this is merely a personal view – it seems to be dedicated more to the glory of man, and man's way with towering masonry, than to the glory of God. The minster is monumental but showy, sublime yet fussy; it's a spiritual skyscraper. I can't really argue with the millions of visitors who are moved to tears by the splendour of York Minster; I can only say that the magic has never quite worked on me. I can appreciate the soaring architecture, but it doesn't move me like the little meeting house at Brigflatts does. Knock the minster down, say I, and rebuild it, stone for stone, at the bottom of Gaping Gill. If that leaves a gaping hole in the middle of York, let's see it as a heaven-sent opportunuity to build the multi-storey car park that York is crying out for.

The Quakers are a community, not a building, and the meeting house at Brigflatts has a more modest agenda. It doesn't make you go

'Wow!' It doesn't make you dizzy with its vertiginous height; it doesn't dazzle you with stained glass or vaulting. With its compact dimensions and whitewashed exterior, it sits unobtrusively next to other examples of seventeenth-century vernacular architecture. The entrance porch bears a datestone – 1675 – a time when Nonconformist meetings were still illegal, and church attendance was the law. Merely to build a meeting house was an act of some bravery: a defiant act of faith that was punishable by imprisonment. When Brigflatts was built, the Act of Toleration was still fourteen long years away.

Toleration: what a strange concept. We tolerate a head-cold; we tolerate a noisy neighbour. But the idea of tolerating someone else's religious faith (i.e. by not throwing him in prison, or stringing him up from a gibbet) seems a rather meagre ambition. We should be celebrating our different faiths, not just tolerating them. Be that as it may, the Act did allow Quakers, and other members of the awkward squad, to worship in their own fashion, without fear of persecution.

Once inside the door of the meeting house, you can take a few steps down to the right, into the meeting room itself, which is furnished with simple wooden benches. Or you can take the wooden steps ahead up to the gallery. At the bottom of the stairs are two wooden gates which, when opened out, create a pen where the farmers' dogs could sit during the meeting. As long as they were able to see their owners, they wouldn't become restless and disrupt the silence. A simple problem, an elegant solution.

Yes, silence is what Brigflatts is all about. You can feel it in the very fabric of the building. George Fox's big idea was that everyone could have a personal relationship with God. They didn't need priests to guide them or intercede on their behalf. There is no altar in a meeting house, no pulpit either. If the Church of England has traditionally been 'the Tory party at prayer', then the Quakers can perhaps be seen as mild-mannered anarchists. No wonder they were seen as seditious; in the business of religion they were trying to cut out the middlemen. Fox had no truck with churchmen: 'hireling priests', he called them. He was equally dismissive of church buildings; they were nothing more than 'steeple houses'.

In 1643, the same year that Oliver Cromwell was recruiting men for his New Model Army, George Fox was a young man of nineteen. As a seeker after truth he left his family and spent four years in the wilderness (or the Midlands, as we now like to call it). He felt he had a mission: a belief that was strengthened when, in 1652, he was moved to climb Pendle Hill in Lancashire. Fox had a vision in which he saw a 'great people to be gathered'. Subsequently, on his travels around the North, George Fox met up with some like-minded people known as the Westmorland Seekers.

When he came to the hamlet of Brigflatts, he stayed with a local man, Richard Robinson – even though Robinson was so suspicious of being robbed that he locked Fox in his room all night! Robinson needn't have worried. From the beginning the Quakers were pacifists, and became known for their scrupulously honest dealings. But there were other reasons why they were persecuted and imprisoned. They didn't tip their hats to their 'social superiors', they didn't pay tithes and they refused to swear an oath.

While the hat business sounds rather quaint today, the refusal to take an oath has a compelling logic. At the risk of being pompous (a risk he never shied away from) George Fox declared that he only had one kind of truth. His 'yea' was his 'yea', and his 'nay' was his 'nay'. Whenever they stood in the dock of some courthouse (which was quite often), Quakers would not swear to tell the truth, as this would imply that they spoke falsely at other times. How can you argue with that?

Quakers are still a force in the world, and Brigflatts echoes with their silent meetings every Sunday morning. You won't find Quakers knocking at your door, or trying to thrust a pamphlet into your hand. At a time when so many religions seem self-serving and confrontational ('Peace on earth and death to the infidel!'), Quakers won't grab you by the lapels and try to drum their beliefs into you. 'Let's talk things over,' they may suggest, in a voice of sweet reason. The world could do with more like them.

I left Brigflatts with some reluctance, not least because it was raining hard. I met a very swollen River Lune and plodded, head down. I wondered how George Fox must have felt as he walked these same fells – with the fire burning inside him, and his Truth to tell the world. I left the Lune (and the Yorkshire Dales National Park) at Lincoln's Inn Bridge. The bridge was still here, though the inn was long gone. It was here that I stopped to treat my one and only blister (I can offer an unsolicited testimonial to Compeed Blister Pads; they do 'exactly what it says on the tin'). Having already decided on another detour from the official Dales Way route, I took a quiet lane that climbs up to Firbank Fell. Near the top of the hill I came to the rock known as Fox's Pulpit. If Quakerism could be said to have a birthplace, this is it.

In those volatile times, any man was under suspicion who could attract a crowd, and George Fox could certainly do that. On a summer day in 1652 a group of Seekers was gathered in the little chapel on Firbeck Fell. Instead of going inside, Fox waited until the service was over, and then addressed the crowd from this rock. More than a thousand people heard him speak that day – for more than three hours – and were moved by his faith. That number included many of the Valiant Sixty – the first Friends – who would subsequently take Fox's message around the world.

A plaque set into the rock commemorates that day. Next to the rock is a little walled enclosure, where the chapel once stood. All that can be seen now are a couple of gravestones and a few gnarled trees, bent away from the prevailing wind.

I continued walking along the lane. The day was blustery, with just enough blue in the sky to make a pair of sailor's trousers, as my aunt used to say. A heron tried to fly into the wind: an ungainly sight. I thought it might break up, like one of the balsa-wood planes I used to make. Crows chased a lazy buzzard against the backdrop of the Howgill Fells.

The Howgills are quite unlike any of the Dales hills or the peaks of the Lake District. They are bare and smooth and curiously rounded, like a tasteful arrangement of huge baguettes laid out on a picnic blanket. This illusion is maintained by the hills being largely unen-cumbered by walls or hedges or fences. The Howgills are not formed from the gritstone and limestone that typify the Dales, but from Silurian slate. No, that doesn't mean a lot to me either. They often change colour throughout the day; towards sunset I have seen them glowing an unearthly pink. When people say something is 'as old as the hills', these are probably the hills they are thinking about.

With the low, incessant hum of traffic, I heard the M6 motorway long before I saw it. The motorway carves an ugly slice through the land-scape; for a mile or two it rides piggyback with the main West Coast railway line. Perhaps we should be grateful that the M6 steers a course between the two National Parks, instead of just ploughing straight through the both of them.

A kestrel hovered expertly overhead, needing only the slightest twitch of its angular wings, in the strong breeze, to hang perfectly still. It's one of life's minor mysteries why we so often see kestrels near motorways. Is it because moles and voles shelter in the grassy margins, too timid to cross?

I stood on the motorway bridge and looked down at the carriage-ways, stretching into the distance. After a few days of footpaths and quiet lanes, it was quite a novelty to watch lorries filled with cornflakes, underarm deodorants and other staples of life in the twenty-first century heading north... and other lorries filled with cornflakes, underarm deodorants and other staples of life in the twenty-first century heading south. I wondered, in my simplistic way, whether all these journeys were strictly necessary. If we didn't move goods so needlessly around the country, maybe we wouldn't have to build so many new roads and mortgage our precious land-scapes to the internal combustion engine.

In the good old days, roads used to go from place to place – linking them like beads on a necklace. Now, to ensure the smooth, uninter-rupted flow of traffic, the roads go wherever places *aren't*. Instead of being slim ribbons of tarmac, motorways gobble up the countryside to either side. They soon become bloated with roundabouts, slip-roads, cloverleaf junctions, Little Eaters, Happy Chefs, filling stations and out-of-town shopping centres sited conveniently in the middle of nowhere. Huge tracts of land are swallowed up in this way, just to keep the traffic moving. It wouldn't make much sense anywhere in the world; in an island as small as ours it's utter madness.

We seem to harbour the illusion that the car is a sophisticated piece of machinery, honed and tuned to something near perfection. One model is currently being touted as an 'intelligent car', for crying out loud. I'd be happier if the boffins could work, instead, on producing more intelligent *drivers*. God knows, there's room for improvement.

People see fog warnings and immediately think, 'Hmmm, fog... I'd better speed up so I can get home before I can't see anything at all.' On the motorway they drive as though the stopping distance at a steady 70mph was, oh, about 3 feet. They've got ABS systems, airbags and side-impact bars, which give them the illusion of invulnerabilty and encourage them to carry on driving like arseholes. Yes, in a hundred year's time we'll see the car for what it was: just another idea that didn't work... the Betamax of travel. We'll shake our heads and wonder why we sold our souls to the car, and burned up fossil fuels like there was no tomorrow.

Overlooking the motorway was a wind farm. Since it was a breezy day, the slim arms of the turbines were rotating at quite a lick. Here is another aspect of modern life that inspires strong feelings one way or the other. I appreciate that these turbines are not the answer to our energy problems, and they're not to everyone's taste. Even within the green lobby, people can't agree whether they're a 'good thing' or not. But at least they look like a step in the right direction. Unlike nuclear power, which looks increasingly like a blind leap in the dark.

I've seen the chances of a major nuclear disaster in this country expressed in terms of millions to one: odds so reassuringly long that we can rest easy in our beds at night. Yet twice a week we are encouraged by similar odds to spend a pound or two on the Lottery. 'It could be you,' as Camelot coyly suggests. Imagine if we marketed nuclear power similarly. Nuclear meltdown: 'Maybe, just maybe.'

If these odds are meant to mollify us, they've conspicuously failed. Nuclear apologists are quick to stress the great strides being made to ensure that nuclear power is safe. We might almost be lulled into a false sense of security by their honey-coated reassurances, until we remind ourselves that the nuclear industry is run by the same kind of people who fall asleep at the wheel, drive trains through red lights and take ferries out of port with their bow doors open. That's right: flawed human beings like you or me.

The people who run the nuclear power stations aren't emotionless automata. They may be lazy or impatient, forgetful or sheer bloody-minded. Their span of concentration can, on occasions, be depressingly short. Perhaps they're not the sharpest knives in the drawer: the kind of people who will spend thirty seconds pushing at a door marked 'Pull'. They're assailed by self-doubt, prone to daydreams, lost in sexual fantasies, and apt to skive whenever they can get away with it. Yes, just regular folk.

They habitually fall out with their co-workers, and harbour grudges against their bosses. Perhaps they've been overlooked, yet again, in the annual round of promotions, and feel a simmering grudge against the company. In extremis they may be pushed to commit acts of revengeful sabotage. These are the nuclear components that give me the shivers. And yet we're blithely informed that a nuclear meltdown is well-nigh impossible. It's arrogance bordering on lunacy.

This isn't just my own personal fantasy of nuclear dystopia. In recent years there have been some appalling lapses in safety procedures at Sellafield. Some workers, too bored to do vital checks, have been making figures up in order to complete their logs.

It gets even scarier. Current anxieties about nuclear power seem to focus on a 'September 11-style' attack. If a plane, commandeered by terrorists, were aimed at Sellafield, I'm told we could wave the North of England goodbye. Reading that in the newspaper one breakfast time left me gaping, with a spoonful of Honey Nut Loops suspended in mid-air. What a splendidly London-centric news item. 'What's

that's mushroom cloud, dear?' 'It's the North of England, apparently.' 'Good lord. Another slice of pie?'

Worse still, we're burying incredibly dangerous nuclear waste, for
future generations to take care of. Maybe we should stick a notice on
the bunker door:

> *We have left you a little legacy, a poisoned chalice. Nuclear waste. It
> needs to be looked after with enormous care. It will cost you a lot of
> money if you do it right, and if you don't do it right it may kill you.
> You'll need to impress upon your successors that this material will still
> be dangerously unstable in another thousand years. Have a nice day.*

We may look after those bunkers now, but who is going to inherit
the job in the year 2022, 2050, 3000? Society will be different, in ways
we just can't anticipate. Nuclear waste will be just a footnote in an
unacceptable history of ecological mismanagement. What incentive
will there be to spend money and manpower in preserving these
dangerous deposits of spent uranium and plutonium? I reckon it's
the nuclear industry itself that needs a decent burial.

In the power generating business, we've got to keep on looking at
wind, water and solar power. I don't understand why these so-called
alternative energy sources are treated with such derision by those
who espouse the nuclear option. In terms of harnessing renewable
resources, we've hardly started.

Once I'd crossed the motorway, I encountered a transitional landscape. Not quite the Yorkshire Dales, but still a few miles from the
peaks of the Lake District: a pleasantly undulating countryside of
scattered, slate-roofed farms. The door jambs of barns and out-
houses were painted white: a boon for pissed farmers, no doubt.

As I tried to find the driest line across a succession of sodden fields,
the light of late afternoon raked the hillsides. Bright and vibrant,
it was almost hallucinogenic. So it only added to the sense of

unreality when I was attacked by a crazed sheep. It was a Leicester Mule, for those that care about such things: an awkward-looking beast with an unsightly bump on its forehead. I was walking across a field, minding my own business, when the sheep had a sudden brainstorm. It chased me at speed, forcing me to made an undignified dash to the stile. Landing heavily in the next field (that's the only way I *can* land these days), I blushed to hear the sheep's mocking laughter. 'Baaaastaaaard, baaaastaaaard'. As I dusted myself down and recovered my composure, I looked around to check that no one had witnessed my cowardly retreat. I didn't want the episode to turn up on 'You've Been Farmed': a cheap and cheerful collection of video clips that's been one of the surprise success stories of Lakeland TV.

With all the walking I've done over the years, I must have seen, oh, millions of sheep by now. But this was the first time I'd ever been chased by one. Maybe it had tasted human flesh, and was now overwhelmed by an insatiable lust for blood. Or maybe it was on drugs. After all, the Leicester Mule derives its name from its traditional use as a courier, to smuggle Class A drugs in and out of the East Midlands.

Sheep may be stupid, but on the whole they avoid close contact with people. They know, from sheep folklore, that people mean trouble – unless it's snowing and they're carrying bales of hay. In truth, sheep don't have much to look forward to. Just the abbatoir, or an unwelcome embrace from a lustful farmhand (or Frank, if his eye should wander from cow byre to sheepfold). Sheep know they're on death row for the 'crime' of being tasty with mint sauce, roast potatoes, rosemary gravy and maybe a choice of seasonal vegetables.

Foot and mouth disease took its toll on the farmers of the Dales. It can't have been easy for them, watching their flocks being decimated, animals thrown to the flames like a scene from a painting by Hieronymous Bosch. It must have been like the death of a much-loved family member. Or, at least, the death of a much-loved family member who had a one-way ticket to the abattoir. But if it was hard on the farmers, it was no picnic for the sheep either.

It's hard to guess what sheep are thinking, or if they think much at all. These Swaledale and Dalesbred sheep have just the one expression – gormless – which hardly qualifies as an expression at all. You could imagine, in a Rudyard Kipling kind of way, that sheep treat triumph and disaster just the same. But what appears to be stoicism is probably nothing more than stupidity. Those concerned about the effect that sheep-dip is having on farmers should check out the effect that sheep-dip is having on *sheep*. At the very least, it seems to make them depressed. Every once in a while, a sheep will be overwhelmed by the sheer futility of life, think 'Oh, sod it', and walk straight out in front of your car.

You can watch pigeons, or cockroaches, or sheep, and wonder what's the point of them? Do their lives have any meaning? They wander around with no detectable purpose – just eating, shitting, sleeping, reproducing and dying. This can cheer you up, momentarily, until you look at all the people around you: chasing consumer durables, meaningless entertainments, social standing, fleeting sexual encounters... and then you start looking at your own life. But that way madness lies.

The papers are full of apocalyptic predictions. The sun is going to explode in about 40,000,000 years (call that 39,999,999 years by the time this book has gone to press). I saw it in a broadsheet newspaper, so it must be true. I'm not sure what I should be doing with this information. Do I cancel the papers? Is it worth buying a five-year diary. It's easy to get depressed. Oh, sod it...

The Dales Way passes to the north of Kendal, but I made yet another detour to spend a little quality time in the self-styled Gateway to the Lakes. Arriving in Kendal from the north, I passed a supermarket with my name on it: one of life's minor pleasures, like finding 10p on the pavement, or seeing a red Ferrari with its wheels clamped.

I managed to find a room at the first pub I tried, close to the railway station. This entailed the briefest of exchange with the landlord; it's one I've had on many other occasions and it goes something like this… 'Do you have a room for the night?' Yes, we do.' ' How much is it?' 'It's £20.' 'I'll take it.' 'Don't you want to see the room first? It's got wall-to-wall carpets.' 'No, thanks.' 'It's very nice. Hot and cold running water. Are you sure you don't want to see it?' 'Quite sure. Has it got a bed in it?' 'Of course.' 'Well then, that's the kind of room I like. I'll have a pint, please. The strong stuff. And a whisky chaser.'

I got to my room eventually, switching the TV on while I had a wash and brush-up. It was 'Countdown' with Richard Whiteley and Carol Vorderman: the televisual equivalent of relaxing in a lukewarm bath. Richard Whiteley has settled nicely into the role of amiable buffoon. Mayor of Wetwang, or something. What's his catchphrase? Oh yes… 'That's the end of Part 1… see you in Part 2.' However much that man's getting paid, it just isn't enough.

The tragedy of being Richard Whiteley is that no matter how long he does 'Countdown' (and, God knows, it looks like he could carry on till Doomsday), he'll be remembered for one thing only: being bitten, live on prime-time TV, by a ferret. It brings tears to my eyes, just thinking about it… a bit like Mr Whiteley must have felt, all those years ago, as he tried to disengage those tiny, razor-sharp teeth from his lacerated finger, while struggling manfully not to shriek like a stuck pig.

It's Carol Vorderman that fascinates me. She earns an absolute fortune for being on one TV channel or another, no matter what time of the day you switch on. The message on her answering machine probably just says: 'Yes, I'll do it.' Yet, for all her money, she still reaches for vowels and consonants on a teatime game show that's mostly watched by old biddies, stoned students and, OK, maybe a few procrastinating hacks struggling to overcome their writer's block. It's a bit of a mystery. What I like best about Carol Vorderman ('May I call you Carol?' 'Of course you can, John. My, how attractive you look in candlelight') is that whenever she solves a numbers game that has stymied the contestants, she flashes a bashful little smile. Suddenly she's not the ubiquitous TV celebrity any more… she's seven years old again, a precocious little girl who's good with figures. It's a little moment of reality in the airbrushed world of daytime TV.

Then came Anne Robinson doing her 'Weakest Link' shtick. 'Complete the title of this Meatloaf song,' she said: 'I'll do anything for love...' And the woman contestant hadn't got a clue, even though I was bouncing up and down on the bed, shouting the answer at her. She got voted off the team straight afterwards. She didn't seem very happy about it, but had no one to blame but herself.

Clean in thought, word and deed, I plodded into town. A night out in Kendal has rather more potential than a night out in Sedbergh. But, as is evident from a visit to one of those multi-screen cinema complexes, a bigger choice doesn't necessarily make for better entertainment. After all, at any one moment there are ten pointless films on general release that feature musclemen in sweaty vests trying to outrun fireballs. Yes, there are always enough big, dumb action movies to occupy every damn screen. They never seem to keep one screen free, to show arty foreign films with subtitles; or 'The first film by a young Canadian director about the love between two women'; or a double bill of Marx Brothers movies. More's the pity.

It was 7.30pm, but the lights were still blazing in a shop that appeared to sell nothing but Aga cookers. A crowd of about thirty people (Aga louts?) were sitting in neat rows on wooden fold-up chairs – just like a church congregation – while a lady at a lectern was trying to preach the gospel of this curmudgeonly piece of kitchen-ware.

There's a branch of McDonald's on Main Street, Kendal, just like there is on Main Street, Everywhere Else. I have garnered a small portfolio of green credentials, so shunning McDonald's should present few problems. But I'm drawn back time and again, like a moth to a flame, by those golden arches, bright lights, primary colours and the plastic wipe-clean furniture, to express anew my bafflement about the company's success. The UK arm of this global corporation has Bernard Ingham on their board of directors (an unlikely boast shared by British Nuclear Fuels), and continues to take over the world like a virus that manages to be both bland yet malignant.

The Kendal McDonald's is, of course, exactly the same as any other McDonald's: the lowest common denominator of fast food. I pushed through the doors, and sauntered up to the counter. I refused to order a Happy Meal, on the basis that I wasn't a hyperactive six-year-old weaned on a diet of tartrazine, E-numbers and sugary, squashy finger-food. I refused to order fries because fried potatoes are called chips. So a burger and chips it was.

Given a free choice about where to eat, why do so many people choose McDonald's? Forced to wait for my burger (thirty seconds can seem like an eternity in McDonald's) I jotted a few ideas down on a napkin...

– Because the burgers are made of prime beef, and nothing but prime beef. And maybe a pinch of seasoning.

– Because it's fun to eat our meals off a tray, with our fingers.

– Because every burger we eat at any branch of McDonald's will taste exactly the same as every other one we've ever eaten. That's quality control for you.

– Because the company has put a stop to the age-old practice of disgruntled waiters spitting in the soup... by dispensing with waiters. And soup.

– Because even for that shortest of journeys – from counter to stomach – the food is packaged in expanded polystyrene. That's hygiene for you.

– Because you are what you eat. That makes you a Lamb McSpicy.

– Because, despite their low wages, the counter staff are always courteous. 'Enjoy your meal,' they say, with a smile. Well, I don't know about you, but that always brightens up *my* day.

– Because this is one fast-food company that takes training seriously. They have deskilled the cooking process to the point where, after a term at Hamburger University, even the dimmest of school-leavers can flip burgers and tip food onto a tray.

– Because the company doesn't allow any weirdy-beardy trade-union agitators to fill the employees' heads with any subversive nonsense about decent wages and working conditions.

– Because no two countries that have a McDonald's have ever gone to war with each other. It's true.

Because the company reveals its lighter side, by having a demented clown to front its publicity. And they've got Ronald McDonald too.

– Because one day we'll look around town and there'll be nowhere else to eat. It will be Big Macs and fries for eternity. Have a nice day.

Waving away the offer of a coffee, After Eight mint and post-prandial glass of brandy, I didn't linger in McDonald's for longer than it took to wipe a greasy mouth on a grubby sleeve. People don't hang around at McDonald's, do they? Being seen tucking into a burger meal is some-how shameful, like being spotted coming out of a sex shop with a brown paper bag, or reading a Jeffrey Archer novel in public. I walked back up Kirkgate, with burger wrappings blowing around my feet: the take-away tumbleweed of our throw-away society.

You arrive in a new place and, since you're on you're own, you look for a congenial pub. I know real ale fanatics who wouldn't attempt this without first consulting the *Good Beer Guide*. But I prefer to rely on sweet serendipity. I always think I'm going to find that perfect little pub just round the next corner: tucked away in the backstreets, out-of-sight, a well-kept secret that only the locals know. But, of course, most pubs like this have long since gone to the wall, or been transformed into fun pubs, or exist only in the overheated imaginations of simple-minded folk like me.

Maybe I'm hard to please. I don't want to go into another fun-pub as long as I live ('Fun? Don't make me laugh'). The same applies to anywhere that caters for children (at least not until they're tall enough to see over the bar and get a round in, instead of snivelling that they want another tiny bottle of fizzy pop that costs as much as a pint of beer; and then, when you finally give in and buy them one, they take two sips and leave the rest). I'm not a great fan of themed pubs. Or any fake 'Oirish' pub. At the risk of stating the obvious, traditional Irish pubs are in Ireland. And I have no time for any establishment that advertises itself as a 'quiet pub for nice people', because I am still alive and in charge of my faculties, thank you very much.

Having exported the pastiche English pub to all corners of the world, we're now busy making them for home consumption too. But I want the real thing. I want authenticity. I want a pub where they make a convincing attempt to appear glad that I've just walked in. It's asking too much, I know, but still I look. It's another example of unreasonable optimism, like – another bugbear of mine – expecting prostitutes to look like the pictures on their cards.

Too many revamped pubs enjoy their best days on the designer's drawing board. Pubs should evolve gradually, organically, through a regime of benign neglect and general wear and tear. There's no way you can recreate artificially the silky patina on the seat of a bar-stool that comes from a big guy transferring his weight from one cheek of his fat arse to the other for, oh, about thirty years. No amount of artful 'distressing' can do that.

It's depressing to see pubs being changed out of recognition. That's not just an old fogey's desire for everything to stay just the way it was (though I cringe every time that a Rose and Crown or a Red

Lion becomes the Parrot and Firkin, or something equally fatuous. 'Firkin: now there's a funny word. That'll keep the punters amused'). It's more that every change is so hugely expensive. It takes serious money to transform a characterful boozer into something trendy and fashionable. Fickle young folk will flock to the place for a few months, before leaving *en masse*, for somewhere even more trendy and fashionable. Forgive me for pointing out the obvious again, but isn't that what trends and fashions are all about? So the once-trendy (but now almost deserted) theme pub will have to undergo yet another transformation. And here's the rub: who pays for these expensive makeovers? Why, you and me, of course, with every overpriced pint of Tetley's Creamflow that we're brainwashed into buying.

Kendal has quite a variety of drinking holes these days. There are smart bars full of impressionable young folk – looking as cool as the ravages of acne will allow – swigging self-consciously from a bottle of overpriced foreign beer, the neck conveniently plugged with a segment of citrus fruit. The bar staff are specially trained to keep a straight face when they're telling you the price of the beers, avoiding the obvious temptation to collapse in fits of mocking laughter.

There are family pubs stuffed with red Dralon, horse-brasses, miners' lamps, old copper kettles, warming pans and books bought by the yard, where you can be thrown out by a tweedy Terry-Thomas lookalike for laughing too loud.

Happily, though, there are still a few disreputable dives in Kendal where you can get anything you want: dodgy videos, MOT certificates, Rolex-style watches, disabled parking stickers and forged safety certificates for fairground rides. The sort of places where you feel insufferably middle class merely for having no scars or tattoos. Win more than 50p on the fruit machine, and the problem is getting out alive.

And then there's the little pub I fell into, close to the church, where I found a decent pint and good company. Samuel Johnson hit the nail on the head: 'There is nothing which as yet has been contrived by man, by which so much happiness is produced as by a good tavern or inn.' I'll drink to that.

I weaved unsteadily back to the pub where I was staying – the rolling gait due to a combination of beer and sore feet. There was a sign in my room: 'If you use both beds, you'll be charged for both beds.' But it said nothing at all about pissing in the sink.

Day Seven

KENDAL TO
BOWNESS-ON-WINDERMERE

Windermere

In the cold light of day, I couldn't decide whether Kendal is a great place or a bit of a dump. On the downside, Kendal has been transformed into a gigantic one-way system. Motorists who miss their turning have to keep driving round the town in a tortuous circle. I could live to be a hundred and still not understand how this might be seen to improve traffic flow. It might have looked good on some drawing board in the planning office, but on the ground it's a nightmare.

Holidaymakers heading for the Lakes used to have to drive through Kendal, which meant that the town was choked with cars. And now, despite being comprehensively bypassed, Kendal is *still* choked with cars – for the simple reason that people are driving round and round, utterly lost, getting ever more frustrated. Go figure, as the Americans say.

It's not much fun being a pedestrian either; walking around Kendal is like trying to cross the racetrack during the Indianapolis 500. One moment of absent-mindedness and you'll wind up as just another accident statistic. Car drivers in Kendal tend to be disorientated, late for their appointment and very pissed off: a bad combination. And seeing you casually jaywalking ('See that fat bastard? He's mine') might just be the last straw.

But if you haven't got an urgent engagement – or a pressing need to cross the road – Kendal has a lot going for it. For a start it's got Kendal Mint Cake: a confection so sweet that you can actually feel your teeth rotting. Climbers travel all the way to the Himalayas just to get rid of the stuff. But the town's success wasn't actually built on sugary snacks, or even the famous 'K' shoes, but on its woollen industry. 'Wool is my Bread' is the town's motto (otherwise it might have been snaffled by Sunblest, to promote their sliced white loaf). The source of the wool was the hardy Herdwick sheep, though not any more. One recent summer I interrupted a Borrowdale farmer while he was shearing his sheep, by asking him what kind of price he would get for the fleeces. 'Bugger-all,' he said, bitterly. 'I'd have to pay someone to take them away. So I put them in a big pile and burn them.' How sad is that?

Kendal has an intriguing maze of ginnels and snickets: a legacy from the sixteenth century when the town received the unwanted attentions of bloodthirsty gangs known as border reivers. Animals, women, children and congenital cowards could be corralled, at the first sign of trouble, in these easily-defended alleyways. With cross-border raids an ever-present threat, a castle was built in the twelfth century on a hill overlooking the town. It occupies a splendid position, though even the most mendacious estate agent would admit that it needs a bit of work.

The castle was the birthplace of Catherine Parr, who became the sixth wife of King Henry VIII. Considering the track record of his previous five wives (divorced, beheaded, died, divorced and beheaded), her wedding vows must have looked more like a short-term contract. Against all odds, however, it was her elderly husband who pegged out first. Catherine, spared the chop, lived to marry again.

Lakeland folk get their weekly news from the *Westmorland Gazette*, published in Kendal since 1818. The county of Westmorland may have been wiped off the map of England in 1974, with an airy wave of a bureaucratic hand, but the paper felt no compunction to follow suit.

Can any other newspaper in the land boast that its founding editor was a famous poet and drug fiend? Thomas De Quincey was recommended for the post by no less a personage than William Wordsworth. Unfortunately De Quincey neglected rather too many of his editorial duties – particularly the one about turning up and doing a fair day's work for a fair day's pay. Some weeks he didn't actually show his face in the editorial office until the paper had been 'put to bed'. This was probably for the best; on the rare occasions that he did put in an appearance it was only to write savage leader columns that libelled the local gentry. After one calumny too many, De Quincey was sacked, thus allowing him to devote more time to drugs, poetry and the book for which he's now best remembered, *Confessions of an English Opium-eater*.

The *Westmorland Gazette* survived his maladministrations to become the voice of Lakeland. It's got all the local news (sheep prices at auction, terrible; house prices, astronomical), plus a long-running competition that I bet your local paper hasn't got. While 'Spot the Ball' competitions are two-a-penny, the *Westmorland Gazette* has a weekly brain-teaser called 'Spot the Dog'. Instead of a football game, the picture features some Lakeland sheepdog trial – from which the sheepdog has been artfully erased. Using your skill and judgement you put your 'X' where you think the dog's nose ought to be. Fun? I think so.

Kendal has a thriving Arts Centre, in what used to be the old Vaux brewery. I slept through a ballet there once. The town also boasts the Museum of Lakeland Life and Industry, the Quaker Tapestry and the acclaimed Abbot Hall Gallery. Best of all, it's got a little museum that, with its glass cases full of shabby stuffed animals, is bucking the trend for hands-on, multi-media interactivity. One exhibit seems to address the question that was posed rather too often during Queen Victoria's reign: just how many endangered species of hummingbird could be killed, stuffed and mounted in a glass case no bigger than a microwave oven. The answer is: one hell of a lot. You'll be amazed. Amazed and nauseated.

The Museum of Natural History and Archaeology, to give the place its Sunday-best name, was founded in 1796, which ranks it among the oldest museum collections in the country. But one of the best-loved exhibits is also one of the most recent: a re-creation of Alfred Wainwright's little office. It wasn't too difficult to re-create, for the simple reason that the great writer, illustrator and fell-walker was an honorary clerk and curator here from 1945 until 1974. The office on display is the office he actually used.

There is much to admire about A. Wainwright, as a generation of walkers came to know him. Born in 1907, he grew up in the Lancashire mill town of Blackburn, seeing little of the countryside until, aged twenty-three, he spent a week's holiday in the Lake District. 'That week changed my life,' he wrote years later. 'It was the first time that I'd looked upon beauty.' Which probably says more about Blackburn than it does about the Cumbrian hills. His moment of epiphany came when he viewed Lake Windermere from the vantage point of Orrest Head:

I walked uphill and, as though a curtain had dramatically been torn aside, beheld a truly magnificent view. It was a moment of magic, a rev-elation so unexpected that I stood transfixed, unable to believe my eyes. Those few hours on Orrest Head left a spell that changed my life.

He subsequently visited the Lake District at every opportunity. As he was spending so much time on the Lakeland fells, he was happy to take a job in the Borough Treasurer's department at Kendal Town Hall, even though it meant a drop in pay.

In 1952, aged forty-five, Wainwright set himself the challenge of climbing every fell and mountain in the Lake District: a labour of love he reckoned would take him thirteen years. He made sketches and notes – just for his own amusement at first, but later with the idea of combining them into a little guidebook. He did everything the hard way, filling every page with intricate maps, drawings and hand-written text. Unaware that printers could reduce or enlarge pages at will, he created every page the same size as the finished book. He threw away eight months of work – more than 100 pages – because the text was 'ragged right' and he decided it would look better if it was 'justified'.

A Guide to the Eastern Fells appeared in 1955, without any publicity or marketing campaign. That first, self-published edition sold out through word of mouth alone. Emboldened by this success, he completed a series of books – all published in Kendal by the *Westmorland Gazette*.

Wainwright's seven Pictorial Guides to the Lakeland Fells are little gems. The idea of creating books entirely by hand seemed to have gone out of fashion about AD800, once the monks of Iona had laboriously completed the the illuminated manuscripts known as the Book of Kells. But Wainwright could bring a number of useful skills to this ambitious project. He had the drawing skills of a draughtsman (despite having had no formal art training). He had the fastidious eye, and attention to detail, of a local government official. He had the neat handwriting of an accountant – a necessary skill in the days before adding machines and computers. His ledgers (there are some on display in the museum) were works of art in themselves.

Wainwright had another quality that proved equally vital for the task he had set himself, even though it stemmed from an unhappy source. He was a man driven by obsession. Nothing disturbed his concentration – least of all his duties as a husband. Once he had retired, in 1967 – having reached the position of Borough Treasurer – he took to the hills at every opportunity, to escape the claustrophobic confines of a loveless marriage.

Like a craftsman who likes to stick to his estimates, Wainwright finished the books in the allotted thirteen years. Once into his stride he produced many other books too, and found the time to devise the Coast to Coast Walk. He did all this without ever owning a car; the old bugger went everywhere by bus. And not once in those thirteen years did he miss his last bus home. Anyone who's ever tried to get anywhere in the Lake District by public transport will understand what an astonishing achievement this was. And he carried on writing and drawing right up until his death in 1991.

It seems strange to imagine it now, but there was a time – not too many years ago – when Wainwright had a virtual monopoly of the walking book market. Bookshops didn't have a walking book section as such, but just a shelf of Wainwrights. Go into any bookshop now, of course, and the shelves will be groaning under the weight of walking books. There's hardly an area of the country without its guide to long walks, short walks and undemanding strolls from pay & display car parks to tourist honey-pots. Books feature walks for the young, the old, the inexperienced and infirm; walks for those with a penchant for real ale, or cream teas, or industrial archaeology.

To accompany every slim volume entitled Twenty-five More Lakeland Walks From Pubs With Warm Beer, Vegetarian Food and a Relaxed Dress Code, you can hear the sound of a barrel being scraped. The market is saturated. Which is why the Lakeland beauty spots are overrun with walkers who, in carrying an open book as they walk, look like strolling Shakespearean players rehearsing a soliloquy.

What impresses me most about Wainwright is his industry and output. At a time of life when a lot of people might be thinking of taking things easy, he was walking his beloved hills, taking notes and photographs, and rehearsing his increasingly convincing role as a curmudgeonly old sourpuss. Yes, Alfred Wainwright had his faults. When he compiled his walks he was notoriously cavalier about sticking to established rights of way. He fulminated about the crowds of people who were taking to the Lakeland fells – *his* fells, dammit – even though he was almost single-handedly responsible for giving them the idea in the first place. In this respect he attracted the same criticism as William Wordsworth had faced, a few generations earlier, about attracting the very visitors he claimed to despise.

Wainwright's more misogynistic observations could stick in the craw. He lamented the fact that women were out on the fells instead of being in the kitchen where they belonged. His first marriage was a disaster; worse, it was a disaster that lasted thirty-five years. That's thirty-five years of brooding silence, only ended when his wife, Ruth, packed a suitcase and walked out on him.

Yet Wainwright did not hesitate to advise a friend about the qualities to look for in a wife. 'Intelligence is the next virtue to seek,' he pronounced, 'and it is a rare one. It is the comparative deficiency in intellect that makes a woman's claim for equality with man pathetic.' Close your mouth, dear reader; even from this distance I can see your jaw dropping.

I saw Alfred Wainwright just the once. He was in a Dales pub, with a group of walkers sitting around a table. But while they were facing inwards, engaged in animated conversation, Wainwright was facing out, alone and engrossed in his pipe and his thoughts. It still seems an apt metaphor for a man who preferred to have the Lakeland hills to himself and who, if challenged by a star-struck walker, was likely to deny that he was Alfred Wainwright at all.

'I am least lonely when I am alone on the hills,' Wainwright once remarked, 'and most lonely in a crowd.' I know exactly what he meant. During a week of walking the Dales Way, I had mostly been content with my own company: following the rivers, climbing the hills, watching birds, often just dawdling the day away. This was to be my last day on the walk. With only about 10 miles still left to cover, there was no great hurry. I joined the promenade that accompanied the River Kent as it flowed through the middle of Kendal. Another day, another swollen river ready to burst its banks.

By following the river to Burnside, a small town that grew up around its paper mill, I rejoined the Dales Way and entered the Lake District National Park. This was as beautiful a stretch of river as anywhere on the walk. I stopped for a few minutes to watch a handsome diving duck called a gooseander. At Cowan Head I passed a gaunt building, dwarfing a group of attractive cottages, which was either a high-security prison or sheltered flats for old folk. On seconds thoughts, it must have been flats; it looked far too grim to be a prison.

Most people drive past Staveley with barely a second glance, now that this once-notorious traffic bottleneck has been bypassed by the A591. But not me; I decided to stop here for a pub lunch. I sat in a window seat, watching the sky outside turn from a lowering grey to bright sunshine, and back to grey again... all in the space of thirty seconds. Real October weather: all four seasons in one day. I achieved a sort of Zen-like calm, through the combination of a week's walking, a plateful of food and three pints of Robinson's Bitter. In a strange way I felt I could have carried on walking for the foreseeable future; I had achieved a kind of equilibrium, a benign stoicism, a bovine acceptance.

Staveley has a station on the branch line between Kendal and the terminus at Windermere. Windermere is as far into the Lake District as the railway line ever penetrated, though it wasn't for the want of trying. At the height of railway mania, the branch line to Windermere was just the first step in an ambitious plan to open up the Lake District to a ticket-buying public. Until 1847, the year that the Kendal–Windermere branch line was opened, the town of Windermere was known, prosaically, as Birthwaite. But nobody (and especially tourists) wanted to get off at Birthwaite Station. So Windermere it became, even though railway passengers still had a 2-mile trudge if they wanted to visit the lake itself. Had they existed then, the Trades Description people might have had a few words to say about that.

For thwarting these intrusive plans, we have William Wordsworth to thank. Not just him, of course, though his was the most familiar signature on the petition. As strange as it may seem to us today, it's really only during the last 250 years that people have visited the Lake District in any numbers. Prior to that, it was viewed with suspicion as an area of precipitous peaks and impassable roads, inhabited by monsters, mad axemen and spectral hounds with eyes as big as, oh, cartwheels. In any case, working people had neither the time nor the money to travel, and those of nobler birth looked further afield.

At the time that Wordsworth was writing, no upper-class education was considered finished until the Grand Tour of Europe had been undertaken. It was a sort of finishing school, whose curriculum included deflowering virgins, composing lyric poetry and seeking out the wonders of Nature. When their travels were thwarted by the French Revolution and the Napoleonic Wars, these well-heeled sight-seers were forced to look closer to home in order to find the epitome of the sublime and the picturesque that they were more accustomed to finding in the Alps and the Dolomites. This, in short, was how the Lake District was 'discovered'.

The first guidebooks, published from 1770 onwards, painted the Lake District as a threatening place. Nature was romantic, yet terrifying. In the imagination of these first adventurers, waterfalls became awesome cataracts. Every mountain was a vertiginous peak, dwarfing the figures who stood in its shadow. Wealthy visitors fantasised about being shepherds. The poet, Thomas Gray, wrote of a 'paradise', peopled with bucolic peasants, where all was 'peace, rusticity and happy poverty' (what the peasants themselves thought about this 'happy poverty' was not recorded).

William Gilpin wrote an influential guidebook in which he recommended the most picturesque vistas. One of these 'viewing posts' – now in ruin – overlooked Lake Windermere. And Gilpin did not hesitate to slap Mother Nature's wrist when She failed to create a harmonious composition. The first visitors viewed the Lake District as though it was a series of paintings hanging in a gallery. Sometimes they turned their backs on the landscape – quite literally – to view it through a convex mirror. This device, known as a 'Claude glass,' created a sepia-toned image resembling the paintings of Claude

Lorraine – one of many artists who attempted to improve on Nature by infusing his paintings with drama and romance.

Most of the early guidebooks should have been filed under 'Fiction'; nevertheless they helped to put the Lake District on the tourist map. Wordsworth disapproved of the new tourists, and the proposed railway too. That was no surprise, really: after writing lyric poetry, disapproving of things was Wordsworth's strongest suit. He didn't think the tourists would benefit – 'mentally or morally,' as he put it – from a closer acquaintance with his beloved lakes.

Perhaps he'd had a vision of what would happen if the Lake District were in easy reach of every Tom, Dick or Harriet who fancied shopping for fleecy cagoules in a pleasantly rural environment. Perhaps he had a premonition of speedboats tear-arsing up and down Windermere. Perhaps he shuddered at the thought of Bowness on a sunny bank holiday: a conversational babel of many tongues, a cacophony of Radio One and the incessant 'ker-ching' of cash registers, as holidaymakers compete to see who can throw the most money at that most elusive of aspirations – trying to enjoy themselves. Nevertheless, by 1810 Wordsworth had written his own *Guide to the Lakes*, proving that the old rogue wasn't averse to making a few bob from tourism himself.

The book was quite a hit, dwarfing the sales of his poetry. There's a story (it's probably apocryphal, but I'd like to think it was true) that a clergyman once asked Wordsworth if he'd written anything else. The story makes no mention of Wordsworth's reply, but you can almost hear him spluttering.

The poet was scathing about the new industrialists who, having made their piles from the cotton mills of East Lancashire and the woollen mills of West Yorkshire, came to the Lake District to build their ostentatious palaces. And when they came it was on the shores of Lake Windermere that they built their rural retreats. One of the most luxurious mansions (now the Belsfield Hotel, overlooking Bowness Bay) was the home of Henry William Schneider, chairman of the Barrow Shipworks. He began every working day by strolling down to the lake, followed – at a respectful distance – by his butler carrying a breakfast tray. Schneider boarded his steam yacht, the *Esperance*, and enjoyed a leisurely breakfast afloat, as his crew delivered him to Lakeside, at the southern extremity of the lake. Schneider transferred to a private carriage on his very own railway, for the scenic route along the coast to his office in Barrow-in-Furness. Now *that's* what I call commuting.

William Wordsworth was even-handed with his disdain; the working classes, too, attracted his opprobrium. He liked to see peasants toiling in the fields. They added scale and a little local colour to the Lakeland scene. But if all the world's a stage, he preferred his yokels to have non-speaking roles. All he really approved of was the literary gentility: men of lofty ideals, who could nevertheless live the simple life. Men, that is, like himself.

This is how it has been in the Lake District ever since; once they have found a toe-hold in this beautiful landscape, most people try to pull up the drawbridge after them. They may claim to have high-minded reasons (and Wordsworth had them in spades), but it was mostly to maintain property values and to keep out the riff-raff.

It took more than one irascible poet, though, to keep the riff-raff out of the Lake District. They came by rail, pouring out of Windermere station in their thousands. People who had never even read Wordsworth's poems (except the one about daffodils, of course, or at least the first couple of lines). No wonder the Lakes Poets took to laudanum with such unabashed enthusiasm.

Wordsworth's big idea, in landscape terms, was to envisage the Lake District as, 'a sort of national property in which every man has a right and interest who has an eye to perceive and a heart to enjoy.' That's the National Park ethos in a nutshell, many years before it was enshrined in law, though Wordsworth would no doubt have means-tested potential visitors for their high-mindedness. The idea took root, but slowly. We had to wait until 1951 for 880 square miles of the Lake District to be designated a National Park.

If towns such as Bowness, Ambleside and Keswick seem to have sold their souls to the tourist trade, just imagine what the Lake District would be like if it *hadn't* become a National Park. There would be a funicular railway up Helvellyn, and a Burger King to greet visitors at the top. Boats would be tear-arsing up and and down every lake, not just Windermere. The beautiful Langdale Valley would almost disappear beneath a rash of time-share holiday villages. Grasmere would be transformed into a theme park: Wordsworth World. Oh, sorry, that's already happened. But just imagine the tackiest, most exploitative kind of tourist development, in the secure knowledge that the reality would be far, far worse.

This is the insoluble problem facing the National Park Authority: how to accommodate the huge numbers of people who want to come to the Lake District, without them spoiling the very landscapes they have come to see. I don't envy these decision makers; whatever they do, they upset one sector of the community or another. Perhaps TV could help. If an unprepossessing town – Barrow-in-Furness, why not? – were to be commandeered as a film-setting for some long-running soap, then thousands of people could be diverted down there instead of clogging up the narrow Lakeland roads. There would be no danger of spoiling the town. Anything that happened to Barrow – up to and including a pre-emptive nuclear strike – would be an improvement.

I eased myself off my high horse once again, back onto Shanks's pony, and continued to make unhurried progress through the landscape between Staveley and Windermere. It's intimate rather than dramatic – certainly when compared to more celebrated Lakeland country – and I like it a lot. There are scattered farms, gated single-track roads, tiny tree-fringed tarns, copses of silver birch, and bare knuckles of rock thrusting through the grass and bracken. The whitewashed houses seem to fit so well into the scene; in the tourist brochures they are the epitome of Lakeland. Wordsworth, however, thought these whitewashed houses were a blight on the landscape, which just shows that our tastes in landscape are as changeable as our tastes in clothes.

Visitors tend to rush along the A591, in search of more exotic pleasures. The day-trippers head for the flesh-pots of Bowness, Ambleside and Keswick, to wander listlessly round the souvenir shops and gorge themselves on take-away food. The walkers have their eyes set on more celebrated rambles: the Fairfield Horseshoe, perhaps, or a traverse of Striding Edge. Consequently, these lower fells are quiet when better known Lakeland honey-pots are heaving with people (and if you want to remind yourself just how unpleasant that can be, take a day-trip to Tarn Hows or Hawkshead next time we have a sunny bank holiday).

I love the Lakeland mountains, with their rugged peaks and panoramic views. But I enjoy walking the lower fells every bit as much, because what I love most is variety. On this day the scene changed with every few paces I walked, and the light was fantastic. I rummaged around in the bottom of the rucksack for my camera. The weather was the kind that makes a landscape photographer's shutter-finger twitch, like a trigger-happy gunman in a bar full of strangers.

Whenever I have a photographic assignment (and what a fine word 'assignment' is; how much more important it sounds than 'job'), I always listen to the weather forecast for the area where I'm going. Or, better yet, the five-day forecasts from the Met Office. I used to be rather sceptical about weather forecasts. For example, isn't a '50 per cent chance of rain' really just a fancy way of saying 'I haven't the foggiest'? It doesn't tell you what you really want to know: whether you need to take an umbrella or not. But the forecasts have come a long way since then; it's no longer just a matter of examining the piece of wet string hung out of a window on the fifth floor of Broadcasting House. These days the local forecasts are spookily accurate. When I'm taking pictures my favourite prognosis is 'changeable'. I don't feel as if I've had a proper day's photography unless I've been soaked to the bone at least twice.

The weather was getting distinctly Shakespearean. One minute the storm clouds gathered menacingly, and I sheltered under a tree to escape from the rain. The next minute the clouds parted, as if by magic, and a slim pencil of light swept across the landscape, like a prison searchlight in an old James Cagney movie. I just stood and waited for a farmhouse, or a hilltop or a ribbon of road to be illuminated against the gloom. And then I clicked the shutter. At such moments, landscape photography can seem a very easy business. The secret? It's 'f8 and *be there*.' Oh, and 'point the camera at something interesting.' There, that'll save you the cost of buying a pile of expensive photographic books.

I laboured up hills, in the hope of getting my first sight of Lake Windermere. By this point in the walk I just wanted to get there. But there were many false horizons. Every time I thought I'd get a bird's-eye view of Bowness, there was another crest to climb. The true Lakeland hills – Coniston Old Man, Bowfell and the Langdale Pikes – were the backdrop to each new vista.

When I eventually reached Bowness, I almost tripped over it. Within ten minutes of glimpsing the lake, I was strolling down the steep main street of the town. Even in October it was thronged with people. You may wonder what William Wordsworth would have thought of this scene, but there's no need to wonder for long. Even from this distance you can see his lip curl in distaste, as his worst fears for the Lake District have all been realised. In fact, it's a great deal worse than he could ever have imagined. Wordsworth assumed, naturally enough, that the common people would continue to arrive by train. He could not know that, about three generations later, they would arrive in their cars. Millions of them. And that once they had attached a touring caravan too, they would have devised a foolproof way of bringing his beloved Lake District to a complete standstill.

I am amazed at the way that so many people are attached to their cars, by an invisible umbilical cord. They're frightened to lose sight of their cars, in case they succumb to palpitations and panic attacks. Getting lost is a major worry for people who can't read maps; it makes them timid and unadventurous when they're in the countryside. They drive many miles – ostensibly to enjoy the unrivalled landscapes of the Lake District – only to spend their time, instead, mooching around Bowness, or sitting in some pay & display car park with the radio on.

What I still love about the Lake District (and, for that matter, every other rural – but overcrowded – Arcadia) is that you can always escape the crowds. If you leave the most obvious honey-pots behind, you can find room to move on the busiest of holiday weekends. The mathematics are simple... 80:20.

I picked my way through the crowds, down to Bowness Bay. The water lapped gently against the stony shore, and almost up to my boot-tops. This was it; my walk was over. I felt deflated, though, rather than triumphant. I didn't imagine that everyone in Bowness would see a wet and bedraggled walker, and burst into spontaneous applause (Oh, all right, I *did*). Bowness just seemed an inappropriate finishing point for the Dales Way walk. After a week of peaceful walking it was like ending a tranquil meditation session with a twenty-one gun salute.

It's not as if I didn't know what to expect. I've spent plenty of time in and around Bowness over the years. Essentially an inland resort these days, the town has cheerfully dedicated itself to proving that you can never have too many crap souvenirs. I can remember a time when there was hardly anywhere you could get a meal in Bowness. Now there are dozens of eating places and take-aways competing for every tourist pound. Trying to get into the mood, I forked out £3.70 for a portion of the nastiest fish and chips I've ever tasted. I've tried, in this little book, to keep my criticisms general, rather than specific. But I can't let Vinegar Jones of Bowness off the hook. The sum of £3.70 may not seem an excessive amount to pay in Hampstead, say, but in homely West Yorkshire, where I come from, you could buy up a street of terraced houses for less than that. And it wouldn't leave such a nasty taste in the mouth.

I can remember a time, too, when the boatyards of Bowness were full of men in grubby overalls, with dirt under their fingernails, who actually built and repaired boats. Now, these same boatyards have been converted into smart salesrooms, full of sleek, sexy speedboats. Luxurious craft that will do the required job of making other lake-users purse their lips in envy. The men wear business suits – not overalls – and sit at desks punching pocket calculators, until some starry-eyed punter starts eyeing up a boat. They didn't bother to give me the sales patter, though, as I strolled around one salesroom. It took only a glance to register that a guy with muddy boots and a laden rucksack was probably just getting out of the rain, and wasn't in the market for a Bayliner launch with radar, auto-pilot and sleeping accommodation for six.

These showrooms are changing yet again. There's a war being waged in the Lake District, you see, and Lake Windermere is the battleground. If you were being dramatic, you might say that the fight was for the heart and soul of the National Park and, indeed, the validity of the whole conservation movement. Actually, the war has already been won, for unless there's a dramatic turnaround in government policy, there will soon be a 10mph speed limit imposed on England's longest and noisiest lake.

I should have no trouble in nailing my colours to the mast in this particular debate. After all, there can surely be no room in a National Park for all those speed-boats, water-skiers and jet-skis. The noise on a sunny bank holiday can be horrendous: a dawn-to-dusk banshee howl, as inboard and outboard engines are flogged to the limits of engineering tolerance. If this sort of activity were taking place in a controlled environment, it would be called 'testing to destruction',

Yes, it *should* be easy to adopt an inflexible position. But, in truth, I can see both sides of the argument. After all, the speedboats didn't just arrive one sunny day, like a flock of wintering geese. Year by year the economy of the immediate area became increasingly reliant on tourism, mostly based around water sports. There was money to be made, and that's just about as persuasive an argument as most people ever need. For years the decision makers in the National Park Authority allowed – if only by default – this traffic in motor boats to continue. And any response to the problem is a rearguard action, because too many people have invested in Windermere for it ever to revert to a scene that William Wordsworth might recognise.

I claim a family connection. My mother was the first person to water-ski on Windermere, and a sepia-toned photograph, taken from the towing boat, celebrates the occasion. It depicts a blonde young woman skimming effortlessly across the glassy water of an otherwise empty lake. And that's what it was like on the lake until all the, er, riff-raff arrived.

I've done a bit of water-skiing myself. I know it's irritating to watch neoprene-clad show-offs doing fancy tricks. But when that show-off is *you*... well, that's a different matter. Anyway, I was never any good. And every time I thought I *was* ('I wonder what would happen if I tried to ski backwards?') my world would suddenly turn green and bubbly, as I came to the surface winded and waterlogged. Would it destroy my environmental credibility to admit that water-skiing on Windermere is just about the most fun a person can have? And, once he'd got over his initial resistance to the idea, I'm sure that William Wordsworth would have loved it too.

As crowded as Bowness was, on this October day, there was a distinct 'end of season' feeling about the place. For months the pubs would have been full of punters in spendthrift holiday mood. People on holiday are loathe to complain, so publicans can charge more or less what they want. 'Splash of lime, guv? That'll be, oh, £2.50. Small bottle of tonic? Let's see, a fiver.' Civility is off the menu during those lazy, hazy days of summer. 'Real ale? Real ale? Of course it's all real ale. It's not just a figment of my imagination, is it? Now piss off, the lot of you.' With more business than they need, Lakeland publicans can afford to be rude and bloody-minded. They can bar the scruffier locals for the duration of the tourist season.

By October, though, visitor numbers are on the slide. The pub land-lords need to win back the custom of the local farmers, plough-jock-eys, hired hands, senior citizens and disaffected youth: the very peo-ple who have been least welcome during the heady summer months. Into winter storage go the patio furniture, the colourful umbrellas and the over-priced menus with their flowery euphemisms (*poisson, pommes frites avec pois mushy*). Back come the pool table, the dart-board and the man-sized chip butties. The pub landlords of Bowness will have to endure the more robust behaviour of this boisterous clientele... but only until the following Easter, when, with a huge sigh of relief, they can tell them all to piss off once again.

Yes, the surliness of a Lakeland publican is something to behold. As I rested my weary legs in one of the town's more salubrious pubs, a little group of holidaymakers was sitting at a nearby table, chirruping away like birds. They were so happy to be here – to see the lakes and the mountains and anything related to Beatrix Potter. One of the women, still in a dizzily conversational mood, went up to the bar to order more drinks. As the landlord pulled pints and poured spritzers, the lady rhapsodised about what a great time she was having. He only had to be tolerably amenable, and the lady would have been charmed. Even by the most cynical reckoning, it surely made good commercial sense to humour her for a few moments. But no, he just couldn't be arsed. He turned his back on her without a word, dropped her money into his till and went back to reading his copy of Miserable Bastard Monthly. He looked like an early contender for the title of 'surliest pub landlord of the twenty-first century'. Other landlords must know that he's the man to beat.

What bothers me most about a place like Bowness is the naked greed of the people who take your money. Instead of welcoming with open arms the stream of holidaymakers coming into their establishments with an expression that says 'I've got a Barclaycard and I haven't a bloody clue,' the retailers are sullen and ungracious. If I'm going to be comprehensively fleeced in a shit-heap like Bowness, I'd prefer it to be done with a warm smile and a firm handshake.

It was time to go. I drained my pint, shouldered my rucksack, and climbed the steep hill out of Bowness. I stuck out my thumb and within five minutes a car had stopped. 'Where are you going?' the driver said. 'Anywhere but here,' I replied, as I eased my weary bones into the passenger seat.